The Achievement
of Shakespeare's
Measure for Measure

The Achievement of Shakespeare's *Measure for Measure*

By DAVID LLOYD STEVENSON

Cornell University Press

ITHACA, NEW YORK

Copyright © 1966 by Cornell University

CORNELL UNIVERSITY PRESS

First published 1966

Library of Congress Catalog Card Number: 66-23405

PRINTED IN THE UNITED STATES OF AMERICA
BY W. F. HUMPHREY PRESS
BOUND BY VAIL-BALLOU PRESS, INC.

TO
J. T. S.

Acknowledgments

I SHOULD like to acknowledge the help afforded me at the inception of this study by a summer grant from the Folger Shakespeare Library in Washington, and by another such grant from the Henry E. Huntington Library and Art Gallery in San Marino, California. These grants enabled me to take advantage of the invaluable resources of these two great libraries. I should also like to acknowledge the courtesy of Professor Mark Schorer, who, in the penultimate stages of this study, made available to me precious office space at Berkeley, where I could work in extremely pleasant surroundings and without interruption.

I wish to thank my wife Joan Stevenson, Mr. Herbert Gold, and Mrs. Crede Calhoun for their careful readings of this study and for their valuable suggestions. I also wish to express my indebtedness to the late E. M. W. Tillyard, Master of Jesus College, Cambridge, and to Professor William A. Sylvester, University of Buffalo, for their discussions of *Measure for Measure* with me which have helped greatly in clarifying my own views of this play.

I should like to acknowledge the courtesy of Professor D. C. Allen, who has given me permission to reprint material in somewhat altered form from essays of mine which originally appeared in *ELH, A Journal of English Literary History* (Vols. XXIII and XXVI).

It will be obvious to anyone who knows F. R. Leavis' brilliant and illuminating essay on *Measure for Measure* that he has, in part, anticipated some of the views elaborated in my study. I wish to acknowledge my debt to the insights of this essay.

All references to lines in Shakespeare are to Neilson and Hill's edition of the plays.

D. L. S.

Hunter College
The City University of New York
March 1966

Contents

The Achievement
of Shakespeare's
Measure for Measure

Introduction

TWENTIETH-CENTURY Shakespearean scholarship
has given us a voluminous comment on *Measure for Measure* and has quite obviously rescued the play from the
oblivion into which it had fallen in the nineteenth century.
Yet it has been comment that has, for the most part, refused
to look at *Measure for Measure* as a self-contained literary
achievement. It has taken as an established principle of its
discourse that the play must be viewed as one in which
fundamental intentions and purport are blurred by a
faulty construction or at the least are peculiarly obscure
and difficult to name. F. R. Leavis has voiced the only
major contemporary dissent to such limiting views, I think,
in his reply[1] to an essay by L. C. Knights in which the
latter had accepted as self-evident and beyond discussion
an "admitted unsatisfactoriness"[2] at the heart of the play.
T. S. Eliot, almost half a century ago, had linked *Measure
for Measure* with *Hamlet* as dramas in some way unsuccessful because of " 'intractable' material"[3] imbedded in them.

[1]"The Greatness of *Measure for Measure*," in *The Importance of
Scrutiny*, ed. Eric Bentley (New York, 1948), pp. 150–162.

[2]"The Ambiguity of *Measure for Measure*," in *The Importance of
Scrutiny*, p. 150.

[3]"Hamlet and His Problems," *The Sacred Wood* (New York, 1960),
p. 99.

Roy W. Battenhouse's more recent and highly influential theological critique of *Measure for Measure* rests upon his assumption that it must be taken as a parable needing "an interpretation to be brought to it from without, since it does not contain its interpretation within itself."[4] Mary Lascelles, in the introduction to her book on this play, insists that no one "has ever read or seen *Measure for Measure* without experiencing some bewilderment."[5] And despite an occasional restatement of Leavis' position (e.g., in S. Nagarajan's succinct prefatory evaluation in his recent edition of *Measure for Measure*[6]), the assumption of "something wrong with it" is so much a tradition of our criticism that current articles continue to assume as a matter of course some basic confusion in its dramatic intentions.[7]

This modern insistence that *Measure for Measure* is either flawed or obscure (or both) would have seemed very odd to eighteenth- and nineteenth-century critics, many of whom, to be sure, did not like the play because they did not approve its way of looking at human frailty. And it would have seemed more than strange to its eighteenth-

[4]*"Measure for Measure* and Christian Doctrine of Atonement," *PMLA*, LXI (1946), 1053.

[5]*Shakespeare's "Measure for Measure"* (London, 1953), p. 1.

[6]*Measure for Measure,* The Signet Classic Shakespeare, ed. S. Nagarajan (New York, 1964), pp. xxi–xxxi.

[7]E.g., Eileen Mackay, *"Measure for Measure,"* SQ XIV (1963), 109: "It is acknowledged, even by those who most admire it, that *Measure for Measure* is a difficult play; and its inherent problems are further complicated by a text so corrupt and abridged [!] as to be in part unintelligible." See also Lawrence Sargent Hall, "Isabella's Angry Ape," *SQ*, XV (1964), 158: Hall refers to the play's "intractable material [which]...may have been due in large measure to [Shakespeare's] philosophical ambivalence."

century audience, for whom it was a relatively popular play. This insistence, however, has produced luxuriant thickets of exegesis in our learned journals by tempting critics to treat *Measure for Measure* as a small island of Jacobean thought and sensibility, penetrable only by the expert literary historian. This way of regarding *Measure for Measure* has limited what Leavis has described as one of the "most consummate and convincing of Shakespeare's achievements"[8] to the status of an historical-theatrical document or, as analyzed by its most determined theological critics, to the status of a Jacobean religious homily wearing the guise of a play. It is this demand that *Measure for Measure* be understandable only in proportion to our awareness of one or another of its historically recoverable elements that has kept it, unlike Shakespeare's other works, isolated and inaccessible to full aesthetic appraisal.

The twentieth century has shown a critical obsession with *Measure for Measure* suggesting, by indirection, that as a play it must have deeply probing, tentacular roots penetrating significant areas of human experience. But the relentless flood of articles, each one seeking just once more to ascertain what is viable in it and what is not, has failed to open up fully the areas of experience with which it is involved. Such articles have given us competing, mutually contradictory, and partial views. Therefore, a critic who refuses to accept as presumptive fact that *Measure for Measure* is a drama *manqué* cannot make do with mere authoritarian dissent. If he considers *Measure for Measure* to be, as Leavis puts it, "one of the very greatest of the plays,"[9] one in which perceptions and feelings of the highest poten-

---

[8]"The Greatness of *Measure for Measure*," p. 150.
[9]*Ibid.*

cy are successfully caught in the tight net of the play's design, his task is far more rigorous. He is under obligation to substantiate his views fully, and with no less than an analysis of all the major dramatic components out of which the play is structured. He must accept the burden of such an analysis in order to demonstrate the nature of those perceptions and feelings that the play actually does set in motion and out of which his high evaluation of the play emerges. This is the task I have set myself in this book.

It is, no doubt, impossible to document literary greatness. The best that one can do is to make very clear the relevancies by which one has arrived at a conviction of greatness. Thus I would argue that *Measure for Measure*'s very impressive power over us is only tangentially related to such extrinsic things as its literary sources, its recoverable historical elements, its Christian references. The power of the play is directly related to the play *qua* play, to its outward and evident dramatic design which involves us with a complex but apparent series of ironies and reversals both in plot and in character. It is also directly related to what one might call the play's inward revelations, to its strong undercurrents of implication in regard to problems of moral behavior and human choice that invite our emotional concern and our half-cognitive "knowing."

This present study, therefore, is an attempt to explore as fully as possible the ways in which *Measure for Measure* does induce in us its perceptual or cognitive impulses.[10] It is also an attempt to define and discuss the nature of the

[10]Cf. John Crowe Ransome's observation that "science gratifies a rational or practical impulse and exhibits the minimum of perception," but that art "gratifies a perceptual impulse and exhibits the minimum of reason" ("Poetry: A Note in Ontology," in *Critiques and Essays in Criticism,* ed. R. W. Stallman [New York, 1949], p. 40).

revelatory illuminations that it has conjured into existence. It is only by such procedures, I think, that one can establish a sufficient referent for admiration of this play and for conviction of its greatness. A truly sufficient demonstration of the play's means in relation to its ends should bring us, at last, to a valid estimate of its stature, to what Mark Schorer has defined, in an acute phrase, as the "achieved content"[11] of a work of art.

My own view, as elaborated in this study, is that *Measure for Measure* is a brilliant, self-contained artistic achievement which carries its meaning within its own dramatic design. I have argued that the impulses it teases alive strike deeply, and with great subtlety and range, into our covert, wordless knowledge of the role of sex in men's lives, into our sense of the human being's endless liability to desire, our sense of the devious ways in which physical lust interpenetrates and controls other more apparent motives, and dominates rational thought. Shakespeare had moved into this area before, in his early *Rape of Lucrece,* in some of the sonnets, and in his depiction of Hamlet both in his relationship to Ophelia and to his mother. *Measure for Measure* is not an overt study in sexuality, to be sure. I should call it, rather, an intellectual comedy with a clear, firm dramatic structure designed to release or unlock our inner world of sexual "knowing" and our inner world of noninstitutionalized moral cognition and judgment. And it is precisely the noninstitutionalized nature of the cognition it awakens, I take it, that some of its critics, from the eighteenth century down to the present, have recognized and found unbearably disturbing.

As a means of presenting my views, I have sorted out for a separate discussion in the opening chapter the unusual

[11]"Technique as Discovery," *Hudson Review,* I (1948), 67.

schematic structure of *Measure for Measure*. In the chapter
following, I have analyzed the nature of the play's strate-
gies, scene by scene, whereby it makes its subtle and powerful appeal to levels of awareness of the human condition
we rarely acknowledge at the conventional level of our
daily existence. I have followed these chapters with a third
one analyzing fundamental patterns in the major critical
resistances and reactions to the play, from the seventeenth
century down to our own. The intensity of these reactions
is highly significant, I feel, as a demonstration of the genuine impact on the sensibilities which *Measure for Measure*
has continually made. These reactions also show the sub-
jection of the play to the vagaries of time and explain the
origins of our contemporary, and misleading, concern with
its so-called difficulties. In a fourth chapter I have evaluated
in some detail the attempts of a neotheological criticism
to reply to earlier and adverse reactions to *Measure for
Measure*. I have done so because these views have dominated the comment on this play for the past quarter of a
century, and I consider them to be both wrong as to the
nature of this play, and at the same time to have seriously
reduced and constricted its greatness. In a fifth and final
chapter, I have attempted to describe, as precisely as words
permit, what is to me the achieved content of *Measure
for Measure*.

In an appendix to this study I have included, in somewhat altered form, a previously published essay of mine
on the role of James I in *Measure for Measure*.[12] The play's
concern with James's views seems to me to be the most
important single historical element to be taken into account in considering the role of the Duke in its structure.

---

[12]"The Role of James I in Shakespeare's *Measure for Measure*,"
ELH, XXVI (1959), 188–208.

Yet a discussion of this element does not really fit into a critical evaluation of *Measure for Measure*. Historically interesting as it may be, it is an elaborate footnote to the play, a way of giving an early seventeenth-century frame of reference to certain aspects of it and of demonstrating the particular emphasis that such aspects would most probably have had in the early Jacobean years.

Chapter I

Design and Structure:
Measure for Measure
as Intellectual Comedy

IF one restricts one's observations of *Measure for Measure* to its most obvious elements of design and structure, one is made aware that the play remains what it must always have been—the most easily apprehended of all Shakespeare's comedies. Contemporary criticism has played with the notion that it has a warped or flawed structure or swarms with intractable things. *Measure for Measure,* however, as its title suggests, is overtly, almost grossly, schematic in its

9

architecture. The arbitrary contrasts in moral attitude and moral decision among the principal characters in the play are precisely balanced and intentionally evident. The plot movement is equally schematic. By the play's special dramatic ordering, we are made fully aware that we are witnessing a repetitive plot movement in which the second half of the play is a replaying of the situation discussed in the first half, but to a contrasting conclusion. Moreover, the play's announced thematic concern is equally apparent and equally schematized, a counterpoising of the claims of mercy and of justice in the state.

So public, so much on the surface is this weighing and balancing in the dramatization of character, plot, and situation in *Measure for Measure* that one is easily tempted away from legitimate criticism into biographical guessing, with E. M. W. Tillyard, that Shakespeare may have been in "a mood of uncommon abstraction and speculation"[1] when he wrote the play. One is also easily tempted to use the schematic structure of *Measure for Measure* as a means of inflicting on the play the burden of being, in Donald A. Stauffer's words, "an extensive tract on morality."[2] But all such reactions to its architecture lead us away from a full apprehension of the play. Its moral discourse, as it centers on Claudio or on Angelo, is neither biography nor sermon. It is discourse kept at a conceptual and theoretical level, not at a personal or at a didactic one. The central moral irony of the play constructed around Angelo as the condemner who is condemned is exploited dramatically in *Measure for Measure* as a moral paradox and not as a moral preachment. The play is so designed that the ethical problems with which it is concerned are made to seem interest-

[1]*Shakespeare's Problem Plays* (Toronto, 1949), p. 7.
[2]*Shakespeare's World of Images* (New York, 1949), p. 143.

ing and important ones to us, but more because they are inevitable in the nature of things than because they are made to seem problems which could or should be permanently resolved.

I should characterize this early Jacobean comedy which Shakespeare extracted from Whetstone's pedestrian drama of the crude sexual involvements of Promos and Cassandra, as a brilliant intellectual tour de force on moral obtuseness, based for story on the familiar Renaissance tale of the "monstrous ransom."[3] I see it as constructed somewhat after the fashion of a Donne poem,[4] made up of a series of intricately interrelated ironies and reversals, held together by the twin themes of mercy and justice, and resolved by a final balancing out of paradox. Its most obvious structural affinities are certainly far less with Shakespeare's own Elizabethan romantic comedies and love-game comedies than with Jonson's satiric ones (as has been carefully demonstrated by O. J. Campbell, in *Shakespeare's Satire*, 1943). Indeed, as Miss M. C. Bradbrook has remarked, "it is one of the few of Shakespeare's writings of which he [i.e., Jonson] might wholeheartedly have approved."[5]

The characteristic surface effect (though certainly not the total one) of *Measure for Measure* on an audience I take to be not cheerful acquiescence in some "lesson driven home"[6] concerning forgiveness and mercy. Rather, it is the arousal in an audience of an uneasy awareness of the inevi-

[3]Mary Lascelles' phrase in *Shakespeare's "Measure for Measure"* (London, 1953).

[4]As does Albert S. Cook in "Metaphysical Poetry and *Measure for Measure*," *Accent*, XIII (1953), 122–127.

[5]"Authority, Truth, and Justice in *Measure for Measure*," *RES*, XVII (1941), 399.

[6]G. Wilson Knight, *The Wheel of Fire* (London, ed. 1956), p. 76

tability of moral paradox, the obvious result of the play's tightly designed ironies. This is the sort of intellectual effect T. S. Eliot has attributed to Jonsonian comedy, where "the immediate appeal...is to the mind."[7] That is, in *Measure for Measure* the initial force and impact on the audience comes less directly than it does in *As You Like It* or in *Twelfth Night,* for example, from an unconscious, unthinking involvement in the emotions and destinies of the individual characters. It comes more directly from the conscious impact on the audience of the play's turning back on itself to repeat a central predicament in order to demonstrate the possibility of an opposite result. It also comes from a perception of the contrasting and balancing nature of the roles of the individual characters, and the attitudes they embody, in the completed design of the whole play.

It is because *Measure for Measure* is structured as an intellectual counterpoise of moral concepts and ideas that the normal, tragic results of the actions and decisions of the chief characters are suspended in favor of coldly comic irony and paradox. The characters here are also deliberately simplified and made less interesting in themselves than is Hamlet, for instance, or Falstaff, and more interesting for the ways in which the attitudes they embody fit in with those of other characters, or balance out in the total scheme of the play. Isabella and Angelo are given exciting dramatic rhetoric in their great debate over mercy versus justice of Act II. But the lines are rather more exciting in themselves than as the enrichment of any dramatically created and characteristic speaking voice of either person. Indeed, one of the apparent difficulties of the play is that critics have tried (and failed) to extract from *Measure for*

[7]"Ben Jonson," in *Elizabethan Essays* (London, 1934), p. 67.

Measure an Isabella or an Angelo who would yield to the kind of analysis accorded a Hamlet, an Iago, an Othello. The characters of *Measure for Measure* stubbornly resist analysis in isolation from the design of the play, where they are made viable in complementary relationship to each other.

The primary, given condition which permits one to define *Measure for Measure* as an intellectual rather than a romantic comedy is that the audience is forced by the play into the role of omniscient outsider and observer. The simple dramatic device to reassure the audience of its role is to place an outsider in the play itself: the detached, rather aloof Duke of Vienna, who observes, controls, and comments on the actions of the other characters. In this comedy, where the skillfulness of the complex design of action and character creates the tone of the whole play, the Duke acts as spokesman for the audience, is its articulate representative in the play. As F. R. Leavis has put it, the Duke's "attitude, nothing could be plainer, *is* meant to be ours— his total attitude, which is the total attitude of the play."[8]

Thus, it is the Duke who initiates the business of the play. In the opening scene, his challenge to Angelo and his arbitrary departure from Vienna create what one might call the intellectual-moral experiment which *is* the play. He sets the boundaries of the experiment by which Angelo, hitherto virtuous in name only, must translate his theoretical rectitude into action as absolute ruler of Vienna, and under the twin obligations of justice and mercy, or "mortality and mercy," as the Duke phrases it (I.i.45). Moreover, it is the Duke who suspends the results of Angelo's decisions to seduce Isabella and to behead Clau-

[8]"The Greatness of *Measure for Measure*," in *The Importance of Scrutiny*, ed. Eric Bentley (New York, 1948), p. 154.

dio. By this dramatic stratagem, the moral problems created by Angelo remain theoretical ones and the audience is relieved of its possible emotional involvement in tragedy, where no one (including Angelo) is allowed to suffer the results of his own folly. The audience is thereby permitted to examine the moral decisions and conflicts of the characters in a sardonic detachment equal to that of the Duke of Act V. Finally, the Duke, who sententiously summarizes the themes of the play at key moments (e.g., at III.ii.235ff. and 275ff.), like the later Prospero, maintains full princely control of the long last scene of Act V. He is in full view of the audience, and he stands for the audience as arbiter, bringing about a final balancing and equalizing of justice and mercy, and voicing the ironic results of his experiment.

In the schematic structure of *Measure for Measure,* Claudio and Juliet are placed by Shakespeare at dead center, and are not themselves subjected to the reversals of the play, but are the causal agents of such reversals in others. Unlike the Duke, they are relatively passive, the objects of others' discourse and others' decisions. In the given condition of the play, whereby Juliet is with child by Claudio before a marriage has taken place, they are revealed as transgressors of the strict letter of the law, not from viciousness but from natural, warm, human instinct. In their predicament, they neither defend nor reject their actions. They speak the neutral philosophy of average sensual humanity. Thus Claudio views his own predicament with bitter resignation when he remarks to Lucio, "Our natures do pursue...A thirsty evil, and when we drink, we die" (I.ii.132). He ascribes his arrest for lechery not to some hidden depravity in his nature but merely to ill luck:

> But it chances
> The stealth of our most mutual entertainment
> With character too gross is writ on Juliet. [I.ii.157]

And Juliet, who has almost no other voice in the play, in her confession to the Duke makes a very simple, morally conventional evaluation of her own behavior:[9]

> I do repent me, as it is an evil,
> And take the shame with joy. [II.iii.35]

In keeping with the intended schematic nature of the play, Shakespeare shows the predicament of Claudio and Juliet as wholly sympathized with, or defended, by all other major voices in the comedy except those of Isabella and Angelo. This is meant, no doubt, to heighten the didactic and censorious reactions of these two senators of virtue. Thus Escalus gives a common-sense appraisal of the affair in his logical protest to Angelo against his severity. Angelo himself, Escalus suggests—with anticipatory irony, preparing the audience for the Duke's measured retaliation—would be in the same situation as Claudio, "Had time coher'd with place or place with wishing" (II.i.11). On a slightly lower level of action, it is the Provost who remarks of Claudio:

> He hath but as offended in a dream [II.ii.4]

and protests to the disguised Duke that Claudio is

> More fit to do another such offence
> Than die for this. [II.iii.14]

And Lucio, the witty spokesman for the point of view of the professional adepts in vice, Mistress Overdone and her man Pompey, makes the play's classic evaluation of Claudio's difficulties in the remark to the Duke, "Why, what a

[9]Kenneth Muir, in "The Year's Contributions to Shakespeare Studies: Critical Studies," *Shakespeare Survey*, No. 11 (1958), has objected to my interpretation of Claudio and of Juliet, previously published in *ELH*, XXIII (1956), 256–278. But see my further analysis, Ch. II, pp. 42–43 and 55–56.

ruthless thing is this in him, for the rebellion of a codpiece to take away the life of a man!" (III.ii.121).

It is curious to note, also, in the conscious design of this comedy, the existence of a number of mocking and parallel repetitions of the central sexual predicament around which all the reversals of the play are made to turn. The main repetition, of course, is that between Angelo and Mariana, in the second half of the play, with which the Duke deliberately involves Isabella, to make her the instrumental agent and Angelo the victim. He also arranges with great nicety to make Angelo's sexual involvement an exact duplicate of the one for which he had condemned Claudio: Mariana and Angelo had exchanged a troth-plight; they had not married because of a delay in a dowry; the Duke even suggests (III.i.261ff.) that after the assignation Mariana, like Juliet, may be with child.

At a still lower, more boisterous level, Lucio and his mistress Kate Keepdown, whom he has promised to marry, and who has borne his child, are a further teasing of the central situation. They are referred to twice (III.ii.210 and IV.iii.180) before the final scene in which Lucio is ordered to marry his Kate, and then to be whipped and hanged. Finally, Elbow's outraged cry, in response to Pompey's assertion that Elbow's wife is a respected woman, and was respected with him before he married her, deliberately extends the parallel with Claudio and Juliet to gross parody: "I respected with her before I was married to her!...Prove this, thou wicked Hannibal, or I'll have mine action of battery on thee" (II.i.183).

Claudio and Juliet are central to the play as the paired and parodied representatives of a kind of norm of sensual behavior. In so schematic a comedy as *Measure for Measure*, however, the actions and decisions of Angelo and

Isabella are the main ones of the play. And as characters, they are paired and balanced representatives of elements in human nature far more complicated than those dramatized by Claudio and Juliet. Angelo, ostensibly, and by his rhetoric in the first half of the play, is the public advocate of the first of the two extremes of civil power announced by the Duke: mortal justice. Isabella ostensibly, and by her rhetoric in the first half of the play, speaks for the second of the two, for grace or mercy, the complementary opposite of iron justice. These central figures are also carefully paired in that Angelo, by the Duke's opening statement, is an announced exemplar of a sternly puritanical masculine honor and virtue, and Isabella, by her opening identification as a novice of the order of Saint Clare, is an announced exemplar of chastity in women.

In addition, in order to heighten the audience's sense of the linked relationship of these two in the structure of *Measure for Measure,* both Angelo and Isabella, on their first appearance in the play, make public boast of the virtues with which they are to be identified. Angelo, having been cited by Escalus as the only man in Vienna worthy to exercise ducal power, self-righteously demands:

> Now, good my lord,
> Let there be some more test made of my metal
> Before so noble and so great a figure
> Be stamp'd upon it. [I.i.48]

Isabella's first words in the play, interlocking her role with that of Angelo, are a contentious quibbling that the order of Saint Clare does not have strict enough rules. "And have you nuns no farther privileges?" she asks. To the reply "Are not these large enough?" Isabella complains:

> Yes, truly. I speak not as desiring more,
> But rather wishing a more strict restraint
> Upon the sisterhood, the votaries of Saint Clare. [I.iv.1ff.]

Quite unlike the protagonists in Shakespeare's romantic comedies, Angelo and Isabella exist in *Measure for Measure* to demonstrate the ironies in which they are involved, and their ironic modes of being are a given element in the dramatic strategy of this intellectual comedy. We do not know why Isabella has decided to renounce the world, nor what has caused Angelo to be an austere puritan. There are no "objective correlatives" for their moral stances in the play, and none is demanded.

Angelo's ironic mode of being flows rather patently from his initial, too easy, too public commitment to honor and justice. We follow with our minds, not our emotions, his reversals, which are constantly balanced against those flowing from Isabella's too easy commitment to chastity and mercy. The basic reversal, or paradox, in Angelo's existence in the play is the obvious one that in proposing that Isabella consent to an assignation as the price of her brother's life, Angelo reveals himself to be infinitely more depraved both as a man and as an administrator of justice than Claudio, whom he had condemned for a mere genial slip of nature. Angelo then extends the dimension of his vicious lack of all sense of justice by ordering the instant beheading of Claudio after the consummation of the supposed assignation with Isabella.

It is curious to note the sheer quantity of dramatic incident heaped up to intensify Angelo's reversal into perfidy. Before his own lust has been aroused by Isabella, Angelo has been warned by Escalus that he may find himself as human as Claudio (II.i.4ff.). And Angelo at once heightens the impact on the audience of his own fall, by the shocking lack of self-knowledge in his sneering reply:

> When I, that censure him, do so offend,
> Let mine own judgement pattern out my death,
> And nothing come in partial. [II.i.29]

In the great debate scene of Act II, Isabella repeats Escalus'
arguments twice to Angelo:

> If he had been as you and you as he,
> You would have slippt like him; [II.ii.64]

and

> Go to your bosom;
> Knock there, and ask your heart what it doth know
> That's like my brother's fault. [II.ii.136]

It is another of the insistent ironies of the play that it is
precisely this argument of Isabella's that Angelo heeds. It
brings self-knowledge to him, and quickens his lust for her.

After the climactic third act, Angelo continues to exist
by a still further elaboration of irony which takes its meaning from his initial identification with honor and justice.
The Duke's original charge to Angelo had included the
request that he take his private virtue into the open market
and verify it in action. And at the inception of Angelo's
protracted exposure, in Act V, the Duke reminds the audience of this original charge in the high mockery of his
exclamation that he had heard "such goodness" of Angelo's
justice that he cannot keep it hidden in his own bosom.
He must give it the public display all such virtue merits:

> it deserves, with characters of brass,
> A forted residence 'gainst the tooth of time
> And razure of oblivion. [V.i.11]

But the dramatic moment of heaviest retaliatory mocking of the Angelo of Act I is reached when he is forced by
the Duke to judge the veracity of Isabella's and Mariana's
charges against him. In so doing, he is explicitly forced to
judge himself, and implicitly, one notes, to rejudge the

actions of Claudio and Juliet. Escalus' premonitory words to him have returned to undo him.

The final twist, whereby Angelo is brought back into a livable relationship with humanity, comes as a result of his own self-judgment. Angelo, the many-faced dissembler, at last stands revealed to *himself,* naked in his perfidy. Against Isabella's cries for mercy, he pleads his own immediate death:

> I am sorry that such sorrow I procure;
> And so deep sticks it in my penitent heart
> That I crave death more willingly than mercy.
> 'Tis my deserving, and I do entreat it. [V.i.479]

The justice which Angelo had first insisted upon was improperly directed against a too easy, too passive target in Claudio, a man in whom it would be easy to "condemn the fault, and not the actor of it" (II.ii.37). But at long last, it is properly, if paradoxically, directed against himself. He has identified himself for the audience with real evil, and really deserves the iron of justice.

The title of this comedy of ideas gives the clue to the ultimate irony that Isabella, who is the causal agent of self-knowledge in Angelo as well as the causal agent in Angelo's public exposure, finally pleads for mercy for her own victim. The title of the play, then, as emphasized by Isabella's plea, suggests an ultimately necessary "measure" or moderation in human affairs, and not merely that one be judged as one judges. And the Duke, pardoning Angelo, emphasizes, as Leavis has noted, that the "point of the play depends upon Angelo's not being a certified criminal-type, capable of a wickedness that marks him off from you and me."[10]

[10]"The Greatness of *Measure for Measure*," p. 161.

The events which flow from Angelo's initial commitment to an untenable honor and justice are easily followed. Those which flow from Isabella's equally schematic commitment to chastity and to mercy, apparently, are not. However the difficulties do not spring from the play itself but from a curiously partial criticism which has almost obscured her role as complementary to that of Angelo in the structure of the play. The most elemental difficulty, at least for many critics, has been an unwillingness to accept as fevered the nature of Isabella's "goodness." Therefore, proper "placing" of the first scene of Act III, the climactic scene in which Isabella excoriates her brother for his suggestion that she accept the assignation with Angelo to save his life, should at least restore our sense that there is simple order in the basic structure of this play.

One of the conventional critical views of Isabella in this scene, given voice in our time by Hardin Craig, for example, sees Shakespeare deliberately creating her as a model of chastity in women as she nobly rejects her brother. Moreover, she is even viewed as somewhat contaminated by her mere *existence* in *Measure for Measure,* and as wholly extractable from the play for observation and discussion, a kind of literary monument to virtuous womanhood. The theological-allegorical school, as represented by Roy W. Battenhouse, however, restates and qualifies this view of her so that she acts to save the other characters in the play from their depravity; she becomes a "holy Isabella, like Christ in the wilderness" who "at once discerns that a laying down of her life in obedience to the will of this Devil [Angelo] is not the allowable answer to the problem posed by the fact of human sin."[11] From such a perspective of

[11]"*Measure for Measure* and Christian Doctrine of Atonement," *PMLA.* LXI (1946). 1046.

her role in the structure of *Measure for Measure,* the great moment of the play is her triumphant recovery from temptation, voiced in the words:

More than our brother is our chastity. [II.iv.185]

Other critics, beginning with Samuel Johnson in the eighteenth century, have considered Isabella to be something less exalted, not because of her refusal of Angelo (which is guaranteed by her identification with a religious order), but because of her attack on her brother. Johnson remarked that there is "something harsh, and something forced and far fetched"[12] in her declamation to Claudio, wishing him death. Quiller-Couch, in our time, finds that Isabella is "something rancid in her chastity."[13] Wylie Sypher has described her as "the prurient Isabella";[14] Dame Edith Sitwell lets her go as "the unconscious hypocrite";[15] and Mark Van Doren concludes, acidly, that "we do not see her in her goodness; we only hear her talking like a termagant against those who doubt it."[16]

Without attempting to weigh here (as I do in Chapter IV) whether a Jacobean audience generally, or the first English Stuart in particular, would be as apt to regard Isabella as a Christ-like figure as would Professor Battenhouse, I want to introduce briefly one other problem in interpretation which Isabella's rejection of her brother has created. Does Shakespeare produce in Isabella, through a gross failure in his art, a character whose actions and

[12]*The Plays of William Shakespeare* (London, 1765), I, 321.

[13]*Measure for Measure,* ed. Sir Arthur Quiller-Couch and John Dover Wilson (Cambridge, 1922), p. xxx.

[14]"Shakespeare as Casuist: *Measure for Measure,*" *Sewanee Review,* LXVIII (1950), 273.

[15]*A Poet's Notebook* (Boston, 1950), p. 128.

[16]*Shakespeare* (New York, 1939), p. 221.

attitudes in the climactic Act III (where the play turns
back to replay the predicament of Claudio and Juliet) are
inconsistent with a developing dramatic pattern? The critics who have argued this theory (e.g., Tillyard and O. J.
Campbell) feel that Isabella involves the audience with
her personal destiny in the first three acts, only to be let
go as a character, interesting in her own right, after the
first scene of Act III. Thereafter, in the Mariana episode,
and finally in being paired off with the Duke, she seems
to these critics, though variously stated by them, to be
caught up and submerged in the working out of the plot
of *Measure for Measure* to a conventionally-happy but in-
appropriate conclusion.

I cannot agree that Isabella is intended to be "holy" in
her actions in the play, or to be morally offensive, or to
break the dramatic pattern. I therefore proceed to my own
answers as to the function of her insistent virtue in the
design of the play, as to whether her actions break the play
in two after the climactic third act. As far as Isabella's
virtue is concerned, I note that it flourishes in an intellectualized comedy carefully kept in equilibrium. The
audience is permitted only a limited identification with
individual characters, and neither Isabella nor the audience can be allowed to succumb to the emotional violence
which her surrender to Angelo would evoke. The play
would at once lose its intentionally and intensely theoretical nature, its rigidly schematic measure for measure. Isabella, in her actions, must be held subordinate to the over-
all dramatic equation, where there are to be no casualties,
where the results of Angelo's dissembling in the Duke's
moral experiment are to be suspended. She must remain
to the end a foil for Angelo, and not his victim.

Her early identification with a sisterhood[17] is surely foisted upon Isabella for the very purpose of creating a character who will not be able to surrender her chastity on Angelo's unlawful terms. She is the intentional representative of an absolute sexual virtue in her actions and decisions up to the end of Act III, in part to act as contrast to the more casual morality of Claudio and Juliet. She also embodies an extreme Pauline attitude toward sex, to the end of scene one of Act III, in a larger world which includes, among other voices, those of Lucio and Angelo. This is the point in Shakespeare's making her a novice and not just a lady of Vienna: as one interested in joining a religious order, she creates a neat balance of attitudes in the structure of the comedy. She is surely not intended to live in the play as Shakespeare's personal eulogy of chastity, any more than Angelo's early severity is intended as Shakespeare's eulogy of puritanism. Indeed, an Isabella who surrendered to an Angelo would be as violently improbable as a Cressida who refused to surrender to her Troilus. In either case, the main balance of the play would be broken.

But Isabella, like Angelo, is equally intended by Shakespeare to be subjected to the discipline of the title: *Measure for Measure*. She is a kind of obverse of Angelo, in which the ironies of attitude and decision by which she exists in the play are complementary to those of her op-

[17]In his identifying Isabella as a novice of a religious order, and in his pairing her off with the Duke, Shakespeare seems to have remembered the character Lucia Bella of Whetstone's *An Heptameron of Civill Discourses* (London, 1582). Whetstone's Lucia Bella "who, in the beginning of Christmasse, was determyned to have beene a vestall Nunne" (Sig. Z₂), and who had defended the single life in the debates, is won over to an acceptance of marriage after the seventh day's entertainment.

posite. Just as Angelo turns out to be infinitely more depraved than the lovers he condemns, so too the "enskied and sainted" Isabella is revealed to be totally merciless in her reviling of her brother, for whose life she had so arduously pleaded mercy. And to keep the reversals which flow from this pair of rhetoricians in complete equilibrium, the play is allowed to come to an end only at the moment of exact equivalence between Isabella and Angelo. It ends only when Isabella has really become the thing she had argued for her brother in Act II, that is, merciful ("against all sense," as the Duke points out); and Angelo has really become the thing he had argued for in the great debate of Act II, that is, absolutely just.

As with Angelo, so with Isabella; the basic contradictions which make up her character in the play are the results of her initial public proclamation of her virtue, and her subsequent public pronouncements on mercy. As far as her chastity is concerned, the play involves Isabella in a series of contradictions immediately after her first declaration that she could wish "a more strict restraint" upon the nuns of the order of Saint Clare. Lucio at once juxtaposes her self-righteousness against the cynicism of a less austere world in his taunt, "Hail, virgin, if you be" (I.iv.16). Then Lucio persuades her to plead with Angelo for her brother, but *not* in the role of an unsexed anchorite who, when sworn, must not speak with men except in the presence of her prioress. He asks her, rather, to teach Angelo, "a man whose blood is very snow-broth" (I.iv.57), the meaning of the sexual persuasiveness of a woman:

> Go to Lord Angelo
> And let him learn to know, when maidens sue
> Men give like gods. [I.iv.79]

But we have already been warned of this persuasiveness

in Isabella (just as we are early warned of the man lurking
behind the puritan Angelo) by Claudio's description of
her to Lucio:

> in her youth
> There is a prone and speechless dialect,
> Such as move men. [I.ii.187]

And William Empson has remarked of Claudio's words:
"This is the stainless Isabel, being spoken of by her respect-
ful brother. . . . 'speechlesse' will not give away whether she
is shy or sly, and 'dialect' has abandoned the effort."[18] It
is Lucio, moreover, in the debate between Isabella and
Angelo, who keeps making demands upon the woman
lurking in the novice, urging her to "kneel down before
him, hang upon his gown." It is Lucio who cautions her
that she is too cold:

> If you should need a pin,
> You could not with more tame a tongue desire it. [II.ii.45]

(In her line, "might but my bending down/Reprieve thee"
[III.i.144], Isabella seems to remember Lucio's pin as the
standard by which she evaluates her brother's life.)

The obvious result of her wooing Angelo for her brother's life with all her prowess as a woman is what we should
expect in a comedy of ideas: Angelo's own aroused desire
for this woman in her, which he voices in sharp and unmistakable challenge.

> Be that you are,
> That is, a woman; if you be more, you're none. [II.iv.134]

Isabella herself belatedly recognizes that the actual role
she had played with Angelo was not that of novice. It is
this recognition, late in the play, which vindicates her

[18]*Seven Types of Ambiguity,* 3rd ed. (London, 1953), p. 202.

request for his life (V.i.449). It is, finally, not the novice Isabella for whose "lovely sake" the Duke offers marriage. It is for the woman who emerges from her to conduct the Mariana episode, the woman who in Act III puts on the "destin'd livery" of secular femininity. (Equally, it is the man who emerges from the "prenzie" Angelo whom the Duke is able to forgive.)

Isabella's initial misunderstanding of the real nature of mercy makes it important to observe that the story is so structured that we hear her voice only as a series of declamations in her pleading for Claudio. We hear it as a series of skillful rhetorical maneuvers pitted against, but not actually winning the argument against, Angelo's own very skillful defense of the justice of the law. Where her brother's life is concerned, moreover, Isabella remains somewhat aloof, almost a disinterested commentator to Angelo on the conflicting claims of justice and mercy in her brother's case, "At war 'twixt will and will not" (II.ii.33). She becomes somewhat more passionately involved, and argues at her most brilliant, against what Claudio had called "the demi-god authority" (I.ii.124). But this occurs only after she has been subjected to the sting of Angelo's contemptuous, arrogant dismissal:

> Be satisfied.
> Your brother dies tomorrow. Be content. [II.ii.104]

When she finally becomes vehemently involved with Angelo, it is not over her brother's life at all. Her fury commences only when Angelo proposes that she who had defended, in her own words, Claudio's "natural guiltiness" so well, herself become what she had defended and surrender her own virginity to him to save her brother's life. At this point in Act II, the saintly Isabella, perhaps somewhat unlike Christ in the wilderness, turns what Tillyard has called her "native ferocity" loose on Angelo and attempts, unsuccessfully, to snatch a pardon for Claudio by blackmail:

> Sign me a present pardon for my brother,
> Or with an outstretch'd throat I'll tell the world aloud
> What man thou art. [II.iv.152]

The violence of this chaste and merciful Isabella's response to Angelo is as intentionally derisive in the play as is the lustful response of Angelo to her. It is the dramatic nature of this pair, at the active center of *Measure for Measure,* to be inconsistent and contradictory in their virtue in order to create the basic substance of the play, the ironies and reversals of which it is made. Indeed, if we need reassurance as to the meaning of the debate with Angelo in Act II, it lies in our detached spectator's sardonic comment on this scene, the Duke's heavily understated description to Claudio of the violent encounter between Isabella and Angelo the audience has just witnessed:

She, having the truth of honour in her, hath made him [Angelo] that gracious denial which he is most glad to receive.
[III.i.165]

The Isabella that we know as audience cannot make the gracious denial that a less publicly virtuous Isabella might have made.

After the Duke's double-edged comment on this pair, we need not conjure up any special Jacobean attitude toward chastity to understand the play's schematic intentions created by Isabella's ferocity toward her brother. The whole play up to this point has prepared us for it by Isabella's initial self-righteousness. We are prepared for the anger of her denial by the *temper* of her previous rejection of Angelo's offer. We should also be prepared for the irony of her total lack of mercy toward her brother's love of life, his fear of death, by our own sense of the need for this hardness, here, to prepare for the contrast of the final yielding to mercy by Isabella. Moreover, we would surely be totally unprepared for a display of tender solicitude on the part of Isabella toward Claudio, for any "gracious denial" of him, in the Duke's damning phrase. We have difficulty conjuring up such a picture of her. It would be a devastating violation of the paradoxical structure of the play.

One last element in the dramatic design of III.i deserves attention: the effect of the teasing quality of Isabella's informing her brother of Angelo's offer. In addressing him, a man condemned to the block and apparently resigned to his fate, her first words carry an angry taunt:

> Lord Angelo, having affairs to heaven,
> Intends you for his swift ambassador. [III.i.57]

Claudio, indeed, is actually forced into his great, dramatic outcry on the fear of death, not by the "truth of honour" in her, but by her repeated suspicion that if she were to tell Claudio how he might be saved (but she won't!) he would not be enough of a man to die for her. She plays a grim game with a man facing the axe, hinting, hesitating, but not quite revealing, how he may escape death. She maneuvers him from his mood of resignation to the point where he will be forced to ask her to accept Angelo's offer (as she had already inadvertently maneuvered Angelo to ask for her body). And the sudden appearance of the merciless Isabella at this juncture, crying to Claudio:

> Mercy to thee would prove itself a bawd;
> 'Tis best that thou diest quickly, [III.i.150]

is the second of the two climactic ironies of *Measure for Measure*. The merciless pleader for mercy is neatly poised in balance with the lustful puritan.

Structurally *Measure for Measure* pivots on these two reversals in its paired champions of virtue. Indeed, the turning of Isabella on Claudio is the turning of the whole play on itself so that real justice and real mercy may eventually win out. Does the play lose momentum with Isabella's reviling of her brother, as it has been argued by Tillyard? Or does the play move into theological allegory here? Neither, I think. There has been so great a fever on goodness, the Duke tells Escalus, "that the dissolution of it must cure it" (III.ii.235). What Tillyard describes as Isabella's "hushed and submissive tones"[19] to the Duke ("Let me hear you speak farther. I have spirit to do anything that appears not foul in the truth of my spirit."), are the intended and dramatically effective beginning of the dissolution of her overweening "goodness," the beginning of her redemption into actual, livable goodness. Her subsequent role as a kind of pander in the Mariana episode contradicts the absolute chastity to which the play first commits her, no doubt, as she permits Angelo to show her the way to the assignation "twice o'er." But it represents her first surrender to a more measured, less absolute mercy, whereby she can come to plead for Angelo in the end, and thus can finally be aware of her own humanity.

Measure for Measure, then, because of its skillfully constructed dramatic design, can justifiably be called an intellectual comedy. But one is left with the feeling that such a classification only partially describes the play, and that the play's meaning is truly in excess of its obvious and neatly interlocked paradoxes. The play has illustrated merciless chastity and merciless justice in action, and has then shown them at the moments of their mitigation. But we have certainly not witnessed a narrow Jacobean homily

[19]*Shakespeare's Problem Plays,* pp. 134–135.

on justice and mercy. The various and shifting points of view toward the passive "natural guiltiness" of humanity at the center of the play, as is usual in Shakespeare, have been dramatized rather than morally evaluated. We have not been called upon to judge Claudio's slip, nor Lucio's. We have not been asked to evaluate Isabella's chastity any more than we have been called upon to evaluate that of Elbow's wife.

The closely knit, Jonson-like structure of *Measure for Measure* permits us to call it an intellectual comedy. At the same time, however, precisely because the structure of *Measure for Measure* calls attention to itself, the play may seem to take on at least a superficial air of rational detachment from deep currents of human feeling. And its effects are rather obviously far more complex and far richer than this identification with Jonson would indicate. *Every Man in His Humor* and *Volpone* are intentionally surface plays (as T. S. Eliot has noted), written to correct, or at least to exploit, clearly defined evils. Our pleasure in them is in witnessing the dramatic skill and adroitness with which the pattern of indictment of folly and greed is made complete. *Measure for Measure,* somehow, strikes us more deeply— perhaps because it ends on a moment when indictments are thrown away, when faults are condemned, but not the actors of them.

As in reading one of Donne's most intellectual, tantalizing, and subtle poems, so in reading or in seeing *Measure for Measure:* we sense that with its dramatic structure completed, the perimeter of our awareness of important things we already half knew about human potentiality for good and evil has been perceptibly extended. The "meaning" of *Measure for Measure* resides, however, not in a scholar's notes on literary history or on theology. It resides in our capacity to perceive the deeply running tides of human rather than of doctrinaire feeling in the play. It is the amplitude of the play's dramatic design of irony and paradox, its demonstration of the enormous range of human response as focused and caught between mercy and justice, that makes these tides available to us.

Chapter II

The Substratum of Meaning in *Measure for Measure:* A Scene by Scene Interpretation of the Action

THERE is an extra and enriching dimension of deeply probing moral concern or moral evaluation in *Measure for Measure* which is not accounted for by the play's neat, schematic demonstration of the contradictions in which its two principal characters, Isabella and Angelo, are involved. The play starts much more subtle problems of character appraisal in our minds, ones much less overt, than those carried by its regimented paradoxes. Below a veneer of irony, the play appeals to our half-cognitive awareness of motives and impulses in its Angelo, its Isabella, its Duke. Like those of Hamlet toward his mother, for example, or toward Ophelia, these feelings have the power over us of the intentionally ambiguous. We are keenly aware of their suggestive strength, although as audience we may find it difficult to conjure up the proper language to describe them.

A subliminal level of communication appealing to the perceptive impulse in us is characteristic of Shakespeare elsewhere. We see it clearly enough in his *Richard II,* for example. The play's dialogue is certainly busy with an intellectualizing over the official Tudor political-religious concept of the divine right of kings, over the king's place in an orthodox, schematized world-order. There is much discourse as to the effect of the deposition and murder of King Richard on the political stability of successive reigns. But Richard, as a character, makes his strongest appeal below the threshold of this easily definable, easily annotated political comment. It is one's half-conscious perception of Richard's deeply rooted anxiety toward death, his wavering sense of personal identity, communicated by his poetic meditations, which gives the play its deepest hold over us. When Richard cries out:

> For God's sake let us sit upon the ground
> And tell sad stories of the deaths of kings,

we keen with the play and with Richard. But it is not because our rational minds are concerned with Tudor political theory. It is because we are made privately aware of the inchoate, transitory nature of existence, and our nerves are made fully alert to the unconditional, unaccommodated man in each of us.

In *Measure for Measure* we are everywhere conscious that a level of communication floats below the surface of its intellectualizing over statutory virtue. This is most evident when Isabella clings in desperation to her identity as "a thing enskied and sainted," and responds to her brother's plea for life by crying out, "I'll pray a thousand prayers for thy death." This scene is reminiscent of Hamlet's rejection of Ophelia, in the earlier play's Act III, scene i, when ostensibly he might seem to be acting to prevent Ophelia's involvement in his quarrel with Claudius. But just as surely he acts to give himself a relatively innocent victim on whom to vent the flaring anger which springs from his own feelings of outraged innocence. Such climactic moments in Shakespeare are brought about by skillful, definable, dramatic contrivances of event and character. But at the same time, they give us a richly probing illumination of the equivocations and contradictions underlying all the apparent orthodoxy of human behavior.

Measure for Measure actually opens on a teasing ambiguity, which not only lasts the play but remains to tease us at its end. It concerns the nature of the impulse behind the Duke's desire to enforce a legal morality in Vienna. He himself has been remiss, he tells us, and wishes his carefully chosen deputy to strike home "in th'ambush of my name." The Duke has delegated his authority of "mortality and mercy in Vienna" to Angelo ostensibly to bring about this new and strict enforcement of many unnamed statutes. In Lucio's words, the citizens of the city "Have for long run by the hideous law/ As mice by lions." At the same time, the Duke professes uneasiness at accepting at face value a deputy so avowedly austere, so much the obvious public illustration of the state of virtue the Duke *says* that he wishes to reinstate in Vienna. The Duke's first question in the play, directed to Escalus, "What figure of us think you he will bear?" (I.i.17), suggests that the Duke is characterized as a man neither wholly at ease with his moral experiment nor with his deputy. His first comments to Angelo include the half-quizzical assertion:

> Thy self and thy belongings
> Are not thine own so proper as to waste
> Thyself upon thy virtues, they on thee. [I.i.30]

This is in part decorative rhetoric on virtue in action. It also carries an intentional sting of challenge to Angelo, comfortable in his untested moral superiority. It is a challenge lost on Angelo, however; after asking politely for some further testing of his virtue, he is careful only of his outward manner and asks to accompany the departing Duke "something on the way."

The Duke communicates to Friar Thomas (I.iii) further evidence of his underlying uneasiness with this deputy, so much the embodiment of the actual statutory virtue he hopes to legalize. He had chosen Angelo "with special soul," and with "a leaven'd and prepared choice" (rather ambiguous phrases in themselves). But the Duke insists upon observing, also, the restiveness engendered in him (and in us) by all human assumption of moral superiority:

> Lord Angelo is precise,
> Stands at a guard with envy, scarce confesses
> That his blood flows, or that his appetite
> Is more to bread than stone; hence shall we see,
> If power change purpose, what our seemers be.

This comment prepares the audience for the gross reversal of character demonstrated in Angelo's behavior toward Isabella. But it also quickens in the audience an instinctive and excited awareness that bedrock human virtue will not be so seriously concerned with rigid, statutory law and that it, somehow, does not ever wear Angelo's look of arrogance and vanity.

The second scene of Act I carefully reinforces the non-verbal feelings of the audience, first lightly stirred by the tone of the Duke's initial address to Angelo, and then confirmed by the Duke's later comments (I.iii) to the friar: this play is to concern itself with moral predicaments subtler and less conclusive than the simple good-evil equations carried by the surface actions of the play. This second scene begins at the surface, indeed, with a casual mocking of easily observable moral contradictions in human behavior. Lucio and the two gentlemen exchange flippant banter over a "sanctimonious pirate that went to sea with the Ten Commandments, but scrap'd one out of the table," and then over the curious fact that soldiers, whose profession is to make war, actually pray for peace. The scene includes Pompey's cynical remarks to Mistress Overdone concerning the uneasy, contradictory relationship between the law and human lust. He notes, using the imagery of harvesting crops and of planning for the next year's sowing, that though the brothels in the suburbs have been ordered "pluck'd down," a foresighted burgher has bid in the city brothels as an investment against the law's inevitable future leniency: "They shall stand for seed."

The main undercurrents of suggestive moral ambiguity and probing in this scene (I.ii), however, come from the somewhat equivocal demands of Claudio on the audience's sympathy as he is dragged through the streets, a public display of Angelo's new authority-in-action. He is both culprit to the law and at the same time its victim. Our intuitive acceptance of Claudio as victim, however, over-

balances our feelings for him as culprit because of the
unstudied simplicity of his reactions. He accepts his love
affair with Juliet, by everything that he says, as a serious
impropriety. But, at the same time, he views his difficulties
with the shame of one caught out rather than with the
guilt of an absolute sinner. To Claudio, his love affair lacks
only the "outward order" of marriage, and Juliet, in his
attitude toward her at least, is "fast my wife." He is to be
Angelo's test case in the latter's effort to follow the Duke's
instructions. But he is dramatized as having no sense of
any great evil in himself, only the conviction that he has
violated nothing more serious than an arbitrary statute.
Claudio's mood is best suggested as one of bitter sexual
embarrassment, not deep guilt. Its epitome is the bone-dry
wit of his comment to Lucio concerning the human predicament of one who gives rein to his natural sexual
desires, to the "thirsty evil."

Toward Angelo, moreover, Claudio voices the outrage of
a man who, while not wholly innocent, has been brought to
an accounting far more severe than his slip. Angelo is "the
demi-god authority" who puts "the drowsy and neglected
act" freshly on him "for a name." And with more pre-
science than he is consciously aware of, Claudio suggests
that his sister Isabella may save his life if she "make
friends/ To the strict deputy." It is his assumption that
as he has been, so Angelo too is subject to this "thirsty evil"
in mankind. He thinks that Angelo's liability to Isabella's
attractions as a woman, to the "prone and speechless
dialect" in "her youth," to the seductive, feminine qualities he understands so well and has already succumbed
to in Juliet, may save his life. Claudio's uncalculated
recognition of the natural, unconditioned woman in Isabella (and the unconditioned male in Angelo) prepares us

for the less publicly advertised elements in both their characters. It is Claudio's view, of course, which finally prevails.

The last scene of Act I gives us our first direct view of Isabella, and both the surface of her character and its hidden potential are suggested to us by it. She is presented as a woman in love with an image of herself in the role of legendary saint, as her first remark in the play, her wish for "a more strict restraint" as a member of the order of Saint Clare, demonstrates. She is also (as she will be with Angelo and then with her brother) quickly on the defensive with Lucio, responding to the flippant tone of his comment on her brother's predicament with "Sir, make me not your story." And she responds to Lucio's immediate attempt to appease her self-esteem, to placate her moral vanity, with "You do blaspheme the good in mocking me"—a curiously arrogant self-identification for a mere mortal.[1]

There are perceptible undercurrents in this scene to prepare us for the discrepancies between the narrow, dogmatic virtue with which Isabella identifies, and her practices as a human being. We sense in her what we sense in Angelo, that she will gladly dispense with any warm, friendly feelings for mankind in order to maintain her public

[1]Compare Clemence Dane's evaluation of the proper actress for the role of Isabella in *Broome Stages* (Kingswood, Surrey, 1931), p. 272: "She lacked passion: he could not get a natural love line out of her. Yet she was not tame. There was vigour. There was fierce determination in her dumb refusal to open herself to the words, to the mood of Juliet: and though she was no born ingenue, yet in her large-featured, smooth young face, innocence bloomed fiercely.... Harry thought to himself that the only part she was fit for was Isabella in *Measure for Measure*: and would have put it on for her if either Lucio or Angelo had tempted him."

persona untarnished. Her very acceding to Lucio's request ("Assay the power you have") prepares for the surface irony—with Angelo as its victim—which flows from her successful use of power. It also prepares us for the much subtler, less conscious awareness we have that it is her initial anger at Angelo's surrender to the woman in her, and her subsequent rage at Claudio for his temporary acquiescence in this surrender, that ultimately destroys or purges the very foundation of her self-love, and leaves her (as G. Wilson Knight has phrased it somewhat extravagantly) seeing her own soul "as something small, frightened, despicable, too frail to dream of such a sacrifice"[2] as Angelo has suggested.

At the opening of the first scene of Act II, Escalus pleads at length for Claudio's life by urging Angelo to examine his "own affections," to consider whether he too might not have surrendered to sex "had time coher'd with place or place with wishing." And Angelo's extended, didactic reply on the theme, " 'Tis one thing to be tempted... / Another thing to fall," obviously anticipates (as noted in Chapter I) the overt irony of his sudden passion for Isabella, given in his soliloquy at the end of the second scene of Act II. But his reply to Escalus also takes us below the schematic surface into the play's subtle prodding of our half-conscious perceptions. Our sense of the moral instability of Angelo is reinforced by his overweening pride in public virtue, caught in his phrase, "what we do not see / We tread upon, and never think of it." Our feelings for Angelo begin to take on a half-acknowledged complexity. We sense that he is too sickly ignorant of himself, an illustration, along with Isabella, of the Duke's "fever on goodness."

[2] *The Wheel of Fire* (London, ed. 1956), p. 93.

The second scene of Act II contains the first portion of the great debate between Isabella the untemptable and Angelo the untempted. It opens with the Provost's plea that Claudio "hath but as offended in a dream." This is followed by Angelo's peremptory demand that the Provost give up his office, and that the pregnant Juliet (whom Angelo refers to in cold detachment as "the fornicatress") "have needful but not lavish means." It is therefore Angelo at his most vain, "most ignorant of what he's most assured," that Isabella confronts in her efforts to win a pardon for her brother.

The movement of idea in the debate between this pair (II.ii) is a curious one. It runs from generalized moral arguments that one might expect to be exchanged between these two public claimants to virtue to the particular plea, based upon the "natural guiltiness" of mankind, which unfrocks them both. Isabella, "at war 'twixt will and will not," first pleads for a condemnation of the fault itself, but for the release of Claudio as its actor. Angelo makes short work of this. Isabella then pleads the becoming mercy of those in power, and supports it by obvious reference to Christ's mercy on all mankind. Angelo replies by turning her argument against her. He is showing a greater mercy than she asks, he observes; for the example of justice about to be meted to Claudio will prevent his sexual offense being re-enacted by others and, therefore, *their* punishment in time future. Only when Isabella, wrought to extreme passion by Angelo's insistently correct parries, drops her plea for mercy and begins to argue that "proud man" is "most ignorant of what he's most assur'd," does her "prone and speechless dialect" effect Angelo's sudden interest in sex for himself.

Escalus could plead in vain Angelo's own liability to

temptation as Claudio's excuse. Isabella's argument, however, carries the day: that authority errs like others, but
cleverly "skins the vice o' th' top," that Angelo should
therefore be honest with himself concerning what ulcerous
evil he has buried within "that's like my brother's fault."
Isabella has insisted that there is a natural, sexual man
hidden below Angelo's exterior of virtue. And at her
bidding the sexual man steps forth with a vegeance. Angelo,
not yet wholly able to accept the truly human dimensions
of his own desires, cries out against the "cunning enemy,
that, to catch a saint,/ With saints doth bait thy hook."
The audience, however, having been made, from the very
first, subtly conscious not only of the tenuousness of this
pair's saintliness but also of the "speechless dialect" in
Isabella and of Angelo's probable liability to it, has been
prepared all along for this vindication of its own covert
feelings.

The third scene of Act II is devoted to the interchange
in prison between the Duke as friar-confessor and Juliet,
who is about to bear Claudio's child. After the flourishing
academic rhetoric between the saintly Isabella and Angelo
on the proper application of mercy and justice to human
lust, the pregnant Juliet is a timely reminder of simple,
gross realities. Claudio, we have been warned by the
Provost, is a "young man/ More fit to do another such
offence/ Than die for this." And Juliet, after having
expressed a natural, uncomplicated love for Claudio, cuts
boldly through the Duke's highly formal discourse on
repentance to utter her matter-of-fact, wholly unsenti-
mental summary of her feelings about the results of her
troth-plight love affair. Juliet, unlike Isabella, clings to no
persona of institutionalized virtue. The natural, unin-
hibited ardor with which she had surrendered to Claudio

breaks out again in protest (and in ironic anticipation of Isabella's vindictiveness) in her cry of horror that Claudio "must die tomorrow!"

The final scene (iv) of Act II, in which Angelo invites Isabella to "lay by all nicety and prolixious blushes" and to assuage his lust, and the central portion of Act III, in which Claudio reinforces Angelo's request out of his own terror at the prospect of death, are the crucial, climactic ones of the play. Isabella's "prosperous art," her ability to play with "reason and discourse," in combination with her youthful, feminine beauty (in which, in Angelo's phrase, she is "well express'd/ By all external warrants") has created this central predicament of the play. And in the surface design of action, II.iv. is devoted to an openly ironic exposure of Angelo's hypocrisy. Angelo is wholly, almost obscenely, explicit, in his soliloquy which opens the scene, both in his acceptance of his lust for Isabella ("the strong and swelling evil"), and in his understanding that his public mask of austerity (of "gravity" as he puts it) springs from personal vanity and pride, and not from deep-seated, private virtue. He himself answers the Duke's initial uneasiness as to "what our seemers be" by referring to his own "false seeming." And Isabella (as the Duke will later, in III.i) uses the same thematic words in her recoil from his proposition, crying out to him:

> Seeming, seeming!
> I will proclaim thee, Angelo.

Below this surface, overt exposure of Angelo, however, there are subtleties and nuances of implication felt by all serious observers of the play. The sense of restiveness produced by this scene, a feeling for undercurrents of implication, is usually expressed as suspicion of Isabella's motives, as in Sypher's comment on her prurience. Or it is expressed as staunch defense of Isabella's own sense of her public image, as in Madeleine Doran's "Isabella's resistance to Angelo is a sign of superior strength and nobility of character, not of prudishness, as modern readers are likely to feel."[3]

But we turn harshly against our own intuitive perceptions in favor of an annotator's need for simplification, I think, if we allow ourselves either simple derision or simple praise of Isabella for her immediate decision to preserve her chastity at the cost of her brother's life. Her forebear, Cassandra, in Whetstone's play, is an uncomplicated woman who thinks she may perhaps win the deputy for a husband by her yielding, as well as save her brother's life. Isabella of *Measure for Measure,* however, has been created as far too strong-willed a person to capitulate to Angelo. She could no more yield her body to Angelo than Shylock could turn Christian and remit the pound of flesh. And she is not "moral" to us, but dramatically exciting (as is Shylock) precisely because she will *not* surrender.

I should rather put it that what we are invited to sense in this scene is that Angelo's challenge to Isabella—that she is as cruel as the sentence she has slandered so—really touches her moral vanity and sets in motion her own (and our) buried apprehensions. She puts her refusal on the religious basis that she will imperil her soul, though this thought has never crossed her mind concerning the effect on Claudio's soul of his getting Juliet with child (nor will Mariana's soul concern her later when she escorts Mariana to the assignation with Angelo). There is no

[3]*Endeavors of Art: A Study of Form in Elizabethan Drama* (Madison, 1954), p. 221.

proselytizing instinct in Isabella. She exists to maintain her own personal chastity, not to entice others to follow her example. As audience, we feel it is her vanity, her picture of herself as a saint, that she is defending when she cries out, "More than our brother is our chastity."

Angelo has not been seduced by a phantom of his imagination, but by the woman in Isabella, by the latent possibilities of sensuality and passion he sees in her *because* she is a woman. And the sudden violence with which she turns on him, demanding an immediate pardon for Claudio as the price of her silence, her assertion that her brother would tender down twenty heads on twenty blocks before he would submit her to "such abhorr'd pollution," is surely her (and our) horrified acknowledgment that such possibilities exist. It is a measure of her outraged surprise that her view of herself as a public model of chastity could actually be challenged. Her subsequent willingness to aid the Duke in tricking Angelo with Mariana, her belated insight into Angelo's motives which finally permits her to plead for his reprieve, are the results of this challenge to her conviction that she should be considered as one exempt from human frailty.

The first scene of Act III is the crucial, turning point of *Measure for Measure.* The play turns back on itself so that the Claudio-Juliet love affair, which has dominated the first half, can be re-enacted by Angelo and Mariana, but to a different conclusion, in the second half. In terms of its nameable intellectual content, this opening scene of Act III ironically exposes Isabella, the artful rhetorician of mercy, as a very virago of un-mercy toward her brother, when her own honor is at stake. It also presents us with the incongruity that Isabella, the young woman who will not risk contaminating her own soul to save her brother's life, becomes the willing and skillful agent of the Duke in his plan to force the physical consummation of Angelo's old troth-plight with Mariana.

It is the interpretation of these twin ironies involving Isabella which separates critics like Battenhouse, who feel the play to be successful only as religious allegory, from those like Tillyard, who feel the play to be a partial failure as a secular comedy. My own conviction is, quite simply, that a careful examination of the feelings and perceptions set in motion by this scene leaves one in little doubt as to its intentions. It is a successful, wholly convincing exposure (and the tempering into something more human) of Isabella's fierce fever on goodness, or her moral arrogance. Up to this point in the play she has identified "the good" only with herself, and as a negative virtue not seen in action. She has refused to admit, even more vehemently than Angelo, her own liability to the needs of the human condition.

The Isabella who, in the preceding scene, had conjured into being the sex lying cold and dormant in Angelo, is equally skillful, here, in forcing into the open the natural terror of death lurking under the mask of self-possession which Claudio wears (as we have seen him first with Lucio, then with the Duke). In the act of arousing this terror in Claudio, Isabella finally exhausts her own self-righteousness. By the end of the scene with her brother, the play has passed its climax and Isabella herself becomes a different, more nearly generous person. At the end of her reviling of Claudio's wish to live at the expense of her chastity, Isabella has lost some of the fierce bloom of innocence. We sense that her recoil from her rage at Claudio has made her capable of enjoying the more warmly human notion of revenge on Angelo, has made her capable of the duplicity of guiding him to an assignation with Mariana.

It seems fairly easy to demonstrate the directions and intentions implicit in this crucial scene (III.i). It opens with the Duke's eloquent and secular denigration of the processes of living; this is at once a rationalization of death to Claudio in order to lend him self-possession, and a rationalization which intentionally mocks itself, as the Duke's initial comment suggests:

> Be absolute for death; either death or life
> Shall thereby be the sweeter.

Claudio, who has not appeared since he set in motion Isabella's "prosperous art" against Angelo (I.ii), continues to accept his own predicament, as he had originally in his remarks to Lucio, in the sardonic tones of bitter jest. He who had been capable of calling his genuine passion for Juliet, ironically, a "thirsty evil," now responds with derisive humor to the Duke's picture of life as "an after-dinner's sleep" in which one merely dreams of the joys of youth and age, unable to possess either in actuality:

> To sue to live, I find I seek to die;
> And, seeking death, find life. Let it [i.e., death] come on.

He seems half-cousin to Hamlet at such moments; and his sharp wit, like that of Hamlet to Claudius, is his way of communicating by indirection his mixed feelings concerning the harsh statutory judgment which has fallen upon his simple acts of love-making.

Isabella moves with ill-concealed, cold anger into this scene for "a word or two with Claudio." She instantly changes its tone from that of philosophical, evaluative discourse, carried on close to the level of Socrates' final analysis of existence, to one of private bickering and discord.

The tone of her discourse leads one to feel that Isabella, barely suppressing the unused vindictiveness left over from her recent encounter with Angelo, needs an outlet for her inner turmoil. She releases it on Claudio as obviously as Hamlet had released his pent-up feelings on Ophelia. She is seething, from her beginning comments to Claudio that "Lord Angelo, having affairs to heaven,/ Intends you for his swift ambassador," to her final savage thrust at her brother:

> Mercy to thee would prove itself a bawd;
> 'Tis best that thou diest quickly.

And the fact that her emotional state originated in her attempt to preserve the persona she has created for herself at the cost of her brother's life, suggests to us what she truly is, not a saint but an outraged woman.[4]

We cannot dismiss the motive for her attack on her brother, after his plea for life, as springing from her high sense of morality, Jacobean or otherwise, despite all annotations as to what some Elizabethans may have felt about chastity in women. It might be possible to ignore the undercurrent of implication in Isabel's harsh reaction to Angelo's taunting the sexual in her. But the violence of her reaction to Claudio's terror cannot be taken as either religious or moral fervor. Claudio is dramatized as a man who has yielded under her goading to a momentary horror of death; and his picture of it ("To lie in cold obstruction and to rot/ This sensible warm motion to become/ A kneaded clod") is so immediately communicated that compassion for him flows easily from the audience. It is wholly in

---

[4] As Harold C. Goddard puts it, in *The Meaning of Shakespeare* (Chicago, 1951), p. 442: "This is religion turned infernal. And it is the worse because of her allusion, in her scene with Angelo, to Christ's atonement."

keeping with her character, as it has been created in the play, that Isabella should prefer her honor unsullied and her personal immortality unrisked, at the expense of Claudio's life. Her anger and her coldness are the *immediate* cause of our interest in her, not the institutionalized "rightness" of her response. At this point in *Measure for Measure* she is the living antidote to all human charity, to all generous, deeply concerned sympathy and love, Jacobean or twentieth-century.

Shakespeare could have created a shy, humble, uncomplicated exponent of conventual chastity in Isabella, a woman as troubled in having to refuse her brother's plea as he was desperate for life. But Shakespeare obviously does not. Her fury is not the equivalent of a simple-minded Jacobean audience's outrage that Claudio dare beg his life at the expense of her virginity. We have lost no moral key to this scene. Nor is Isabella, in her overweening rage, intended as an example of Christian orthodoxy, as an eccentric modern criticism will have it. If one were in any doubt whatever as to the implications of this scene, one need merely recall that Claudio, recoiling quickly from his momentary terror of the grave, tries twice to halt the flood of Isabella's anger. But she will not hear him. She is dramatized for us as a person beyond stopping, even though as audience we see that she has won Claudio over completely to her "honorable" view. She prefers to drown his acceptance of his death as the price of her virtue in a self-righteous anger (no longer applicable), leaving him sick of life itself. And Claudio's final comment on this exchange with his sister, "I am so out of love with life that I will sue to be rid of it," makes this exchange *his* triumph. We sense that he has yielded to no calculated dishonoring of Isabella, but rather that she has yielded to a defensive excoriation of him. Her excoriation is the verbal equivalent of her overpowering dismay that her brother, like Angelo, has destroyed her arrogant dream of exemption from normal human involvement.

One way of making very clear the fact that Isabella's reviling of Claudio is not intended to implicate the audience in her personal feelings is to contrast it with Emilia's final turning on Othello. Emilia is presented as a realistic, matter-of-fact person, with no pretense to outstanding virtue in the small affairs of living. She would cuckold her husband for a sufficient price. But precisely because she does not speak from an absolute, advertised virtue, she can cry out against the murder of Desdemona in a passion of rage with which we do identify. We, as minor sinners all, accept her outcry against a major stupidity gladly. It shows a moral proportion in things, a sense of perspective. This is anger we feel wholly justified in indulging, and can enjoy identifying with it.

But, as Samuel Johnson's comment on the harshness of Isabella's declamation against Claudio suggests,[5] it is moral vigor misapplied, and with the wrong object. An Isabella who had given Claudio a "gracious denial," as the Duke phrased it (a Shylock who had remitted the bond voluntarily), would no doubt make for less complication. But we surely prefer the dramatic excitement and tension created by Isabella's "far fetched" ferocity. And in our preference lies our awareness that Claudio is more violently derided by his sister than is Angelo, and for less cause. We recognize that Isabella herself, in teasing his mortal terror and his plea for life out from under his philosophic calm, acts as if she needed his plea for his life to justify her

[5]*The Plays of William Shakespeare,* 8 vols. (London, 1765), I, 321, note 5.

refusal of it. Her reduction of Claudio (whom we have observed playing the man with Lucio and the Duke) to a person all nerves reveals not a capacity for Christian mercy in her, but rather a capacity for sick and self-righteous anger.

Our sympathy for Isabella, at this point of the play, is sufficiently attentuated so that she must change course so as not to break the play in two (as Tillyard will have it), but to save it.[6] If we were to assume that Isabella's derision of Claudio were meant to be highly laudable, then her role in the Mariana-Angelo assignation becomes more wildly contradictory and improbable than even Tillyard has supposed. But we know that her harsh derision is unacceptable at least to the Duke, who has overheard it, and immediately seeks to give it a different and a more reasonable direction: that of virtue not preening itself in angry rhetoric, but virtue in action. Moreover, Isabella cannot maintain her fever on goodness at the cost of her brother's life and still leave us with a play. Her "goodness" has to be tempered more delicately, no doubt, than does that of Angelo. Her excess has been more by omission than commission. She has identified herself, ferociously, with a virtue which in other circumstances is held by most men to be admirable. And at the crucial moment in the play she therefore mitigates the inhumanity of her "goodness" in the only way open to her. When she tells the Duke "I have

[6]W. H. Durham observes that if Isabella's moments with Claudio "did not reveal to her that she, too, was ignorant of her glassy essence, they should have. That there are within her unknown and unsuspected areas of blackness becomes only too plainly visible to the observer" ("What Art Thou Angelo?," *Studies in the Comic* [University of California Publications in English, VIII, No. 2 (1941)], 170–171).

spirit to do anything that appears not foul in the truth of my spirit," we feel that she has abandoned a corrodingly false innocence. Her virtue, in the Duke's words, has finally become "bold" and her "goodness never fearful." She is, at long last, but appropriately, dressed in the "destin'd livery" of Angelo's taunting.

The second and final scene of Act III, following immediately upon the climactic first scene, represents a sudden modulation of the play to a mood of greatly reduced tension. At the end of III.i, Isabella's "fever on goodness" has been given physic. She has been led firmly by the Duke from her "prosperous dialect," from her rhetorical flourishes on morality where she has been passively wasting herself upon her virtues, into the positive action of arranging the Mariana assignation. She has been readied for her cure by the prospect of an action in which her virtue will, in the Duke's early words to Angelo, "go forth" of her. Now the play seems to relax, to pause for a survey of some of the less elevated, more casual aspects of man's liability to sexual desire before turning toward the complications of its denouement. And the Duke, as the guiding, central figure of *Measure for Measure,* remains on stage for the whole of this final scene of Act III, giving its rather tenuous relationship to the rest of the play the solidity of his presence.

The final scene of Act III could be described as a sort of scherzo movement, an extension of the range of the play's comment on man as a sexual creature to a view of sex itself, unadulterated either by passion or by morality. Claudio and Juliet, for all the natural guiltiness of their love, Angelo for all his seeming, do live in the comfortable world of moral habit. But Pompey, Lucio, and Mistress Overdone, whose comments make up this scene, do not.

Pompey, moreover, wholly exempt from any of the effects of fevered goodness, at the beginning of the scene even attempts to defend his pimping against the brutal excoriations of the Duke:

Indeed, it does stink in some sort, sir; but yet sir, I would prove—[III.ii.29]

Lucio merrily limits sex to its harmless mechanics. He reduces Claudio's affair with Juliet to "the rebellion of a cod-piece," "filling a bottle with a tun-dish," to mere "untrussing" (III.ii.122, 182, 190). Lucio's point of view, which graphically denudes sex of everything but the nervous physical thrill of the act itself, is a brilliant bit of witty counterbalancing of the complex problems at the heart of the play.

Lucio emerges from this comic interlude, it should be observed, as foil to the Duke, a second role for Lucio in the play's design. Lucio's subsequent raw comments in this scene on the Duke's sexual adventures, his "feeling for the sport," comic on the surface, carry an enriching undercurrent of intuitive logic into the play. They form a sort of crude literalization of Isabella's arguments to Angelo that *his* private awareness of a "natural guiltiness" in sexual matters should be the basis of his public mercy to Claudio. To Lucio a complete man like the Duke, in contrast to his "ungenitur'd agent" Angelo, could only have failed to enforce laws against fornication in Vienna because "he knew the service, and that instructed him to mercy" (III.ii.127). Lucio, embroidering on his own interpretation, argues, moreover, that the Duke, "Ere he would have hang'd a man for getting a hundred bastards, he would have paid for the nursing a thousand" (III.ii.124). Though we accept the logic of Lucio's reasoning when he attributes the Duke's former leniency to an awareness of his own guilt, we also know Lucio to be completely wrong as to his facts. But the humor of his comment takes on a curious depth by its ability to disturb the Duke as to his own motives and intentions. Before the end of this final scene of Act III, the Duke is dramatized as seeking explicit reassurance from Escalus as to the nature of his own character (III.ii.244, 248).

But if Lucio's language cuts below the respectable to the natural, if he talks below the conventual and the statutory "tone" of discourse set by Isabella and by Angelo, using the crude symbolism of a bottle and a funnel to suggest that act of sex, the Duke remains steadily aloof and proper. Except for his questioning of Escalus concerning his own image in the eyes of the public, the Duke remains wholly self-possessed and the spokesman for an almost disinterested objectivity in men's affairs. His thematic utterance occurs toward the end of this scene: "there is so great a fever on goodness, that the dissolution of it must cure it" (III.ii.235).[7] He brings us back to the basic moral ironies of the play in a final sententious jingle which brings the scene to an end with a comment on Angelo the seemer, and on the nature of true justice (III.ii.275–296).

Act IV brings us back to the action of the play after the long pause of III.ii, and *Measure for Measure* begins its complicated pattern of descent from its climactic scenes to its final resolution. In terms of dramatic structure and

[7]William P. Holden, in *Anti-Puritan Satire, 1572–1642* (New Haven, 1954), pp. 152 and 150, remarks: "Shakespeare and Middleton...are, in the implications attached to their precisians, not far from the observations of Hooker and Bacon." That is to say, that "excess of change, self-righteousness, and zeal are destructive of order."

design, Act IV is largely concerned with plot, with the tricks by which Claudio will be saved, with the devices and stratagems by which Angelo's deeds will duplicate those of Claudio, with the mechanics of the Duke's return to Vienna. But in each of the first three scenes of Act IV there are additional significant implications below the surface action to enrich our understanding of the nature of the completed acts and the unfulfilled intents of the central characters. At the end of these first three scenes, with the translation of Isabella's rhetoric on goodness into useful action, we begin to sense that all the crimes of the play have been rendered forgivable. They may perhaps remain shocking, but they are also acceptable as "natural" deviations from what is expected of us all in a world of civilized moral intent.

In the first scene of Act IV the implications flow both from the Duke's insistence that the exact situation of Claudio and Juliet be duplicated in cold blood by Angelo and Mariana, and from Isabella's bold reversal of attitude which permits her to be the agent of the Duke's scheme. Isabella in her earlier pleadings with Angelo had expressed abhorrence at what she referred to as Claudio's "vice." At the height of her abuse of Claudio, she had called his love-making "sin" and described it as "not accidental, but a trade." But the Duke's specific request that Angelo and Mariana actually bring their old troth-plight to physical consummation, "It is not my consent/ But my entreaty, too" (IV.i.67), and his assertion that the sexual encounter would be no sin (IV.i.73), takes away any lingering stigma from Claudio and Juliet, and allows mercy in Isabella's earlier phrase, quite literally to "prove itself a bawd."

The Duke's scheme, then, verifies both our sense of an essential propriety in Claudio's and Juliet's affair, and an essential propriety in our fascinated repugnance with the febrile quality of Isabella's initial "goodness." The reversal of attitude in Isabella also establishes the validity of her earlier reaction as harsh and excessive, and is very important to the credibility of the denouement. For if we take her initial view of Claudio and Juliet (or her estimate of Claudio's character in III.i.) as the point of view of the whole play rather than as merely proper to Isabella as an interesting character in her first way of reacting, we are forced to accept both sets of troth-plight indulgers as sinful lechers down to the play's end. Under these circumstances, the Duke's ultimate and cheerful all-round forgiveness would make him and us frivolous cynics. That Isabella is disciplined, as well as Angelo, moreover, is apparent from her weeping for her brother (in IV.iii.132), and in the Duke's insistence that she reach heavenly comfort through despair.

In scene ii of Act IV the implications flow from its linking of Claudio's name with that of Barnardine the murderer. At its beginning, as if to insist upon our proper sorting out of degrees of evil, the Provost announces the imminent deaths of both men. Later in this scene the Provost once more affirms his pity for Claudio, but "not a jot the other,/ Being a murderer" (IV.ii.64). Finally, the two are joined in Angelo's special death warrant that Claudio be executed first, early in the morning "by four of the clock; and in the afternoon Barnardine."

The power of this linking of Claudio's name and therefore crime with that of Barnardine makes its effect below the surface comedy of this scene, in which Pompey and Abhorson quarrel over the comparative dignity of the professions of pimp and headsman. It gives a final solidity to our awareness of the relative innocence of Claudio. In his exchange with Isabella (II.iv), Angelo had already argued that the killing a man and the begetting one out of wedlock were equally punishable, equally "filthy vices." And his pairing of Claudio and Barnardine in IV.ii keeps alive and potent for us our *own* sense of the vast difference between murder and the very human, and to the Provost rather admirable, act of sex a little this side of actual marriage. Moreover, it also serves as a final reminder of Angelo's hidden depravity, his skinning "the vice o' th' top," in his insistence that Barnardine, a lump of a man, truly a monster bereft of all moral sensibility, "unfit to live or die," in the Duke's summary (IV.iii.68), be made Claudio's co-partner and equal in crime and execution.

In scene iii of Act IV the play pauses in its movement toward denouement to explore further the bestiality of Barnardine. We view him indirectly through the comic importunings of Pompey—"You must be so good, sir, to rise and be put to death" (IV.iii.28)—and directly through the Duke's serious assertions as to his condition. Barnardine's function in the penultimate moments of *Measure for Measure*, I take it, is to give the play, and its audience, a further sense of moral perspective. The Duke has represented the truly detached, philosophical, self-controlled person not passion's slave. And we are subtly conscious that all the other characters of *Measure for Measure* are in assorted states of alienation from the Duke's detachment. We are aware of sick virtue in Isabella and in Angelo, of unthinking passion in Claudio and Juliet, of the cheerful face of lust in Lucio and in Pompey. In Barnardine ("He is coming, sir, he is coming. I hear his straw rustle"), we see a man in whom all reason, all feeling, is moldy and unused. Unlike any other character in the play, he exists, in stark contrast, wholly outside the normally perceived daily world of good and evil.

The final Act V of *Measure for Measure,* on its intellectualized surface, moves with economy and celerity into the expected clarifications of the denouement. It begins on a heavy note of irony as the returning Duke congratulates Angelo on the "goodness" of his "justice." It then glides, almost ballet-like in formality, through a series of partial revelations centered on the tangled interrelationships of Angelo, Mariana, and Isabella. First, Isabella steps forth to summarize her injuries (V.i.20); then Mariana, in succession, steps forth to accuse Angelo (V.i.169); and finally the Duke, disguised as Friar, comes forward to join the choral accusation of the Deputy (V.i.261). The emotional suspense built up by the carefully sustained confusion in this series of interrelationships is released in a final moment of complete and happy revelation. The ending is, of course, not "realistic." It attains its dramatic balance, with its characters and its events in a stylized harmony, by pairing off Claudio and Juliet, Angelo and Mariana, Lucio and Kate, and the Duke and Isabella in marriage or in its anticipation.

The romantic critics have objected to this conciliatory ending to *Measure for Measure,* and contemporary editors have occasionally agreed with them. But for all its somber plot, the tone of this play, as it descends from its climactic scenes between Isabella and Angelo and Isabella and Claudio, is as surely ameliorative as is that of *As You Like It* or, to choose a very late play, as is that of *The Tempest.* And in the long, single scene of Act V this tone takes over completely. Its most obvious source lies in the bantering wit of Lucio played against the austerity of the Duke, first when Isabella is making her appeal, then when Mari-

ana is pleading, and finally when the Duke insists that
Lucio marry his Kate. To the Duke's question to Angelo,
"Know you this woman?", Lucio promptly intrudes, "Car-
nally, she says." And he keeps alive and vibrant to the
play's end a sturdy amoral view of human passion as the
sheer act of sex. This view constantly and rudely mitigates
the serious element in Angelo's perfidy by reminding us
of the neutral, mechanical, common denominator to all
love-making by which we have all arrived on the scene,
and by which we are all united in each other's transgressions in love.

Isabella is willing to assert falsely, in the final act of
Measure for Measure as part of the case against Angelo,
that "after much debatement. . . /I did yield to him," and
subsequently to plead for Angelo's life. This new view
represents, the culmination of her retreat from mere
rhetoric (in her words, "How I persuaded, how I pray'd,
and kneel'd,/How he refell'd me, and how I repli'd") to
virtue going forth of her. The implications flowing from
these assertions are concilliatory, moreover, in a much
subtler way than that suggested by Lucio's raucous wit.
They suggest to us a much deeper understanding of the
complex nature of human liability to irrational desire.
Mariana's flat statement to the Duke, that she "craves no
other nor no better man" (V.i.431) than Angelo, adds one
more touch to the mood of reconciliation pervading Act V.
But Isabella's attempt to understand and to explicate
Angelo's transgressions—"I partly think/A due sincerity
govern'd his deeds/Till he did I look on me" (V.i.450)
brings them within range of what we covertly admit to be
the ineluctable in ourselves.

The ameliorative elements in Act V (and in the whole
of *Measure for Measure*) reach their most acute and telling

assertion, however, in the Duke's knowing, witty final comments to Angelo. The Duke has just revealed the living Claudio to Isabella as potent example of the fact that Angelo's "act did not o'retake his bad intent," and has asked for Isabella's hand in marriage "for your lovely sake." He then turns toward Angelo, remarking obliquely: "By this Lord Angelo perceives he's safe;/Methinks I see a quick'ning in his eye" (V.i.499). Finally, he addresses Angelo directly, stressing the fact that Angelo has actually profited by his evil transgressions: "Well, Angelo, your evil quits you well" (V.i.501). This is the most profound irony of the play, an irony of acceptance, what Kenneth Burke has called "true irony, humble irony, . . . based upon a sense of fundamental kinship with the enemy."[8] This statement of the Duke's proclaims an ultimate neutrality, and neither condones nor condemns Angelo. It involves the play with a legal mercy, to be sure. But it involves us, as audience, and by implication, in a wordless acceptance of Angelo as the dramatic embodiment of a shared human condition. At the play's end Angelo has become one who serves to illuminate the private world of vanity and desire every one of us inhabits.

The subtleties and nuances revealed in a scene by scene exploration of *Measure for Measure* enrich the play far beyond its surface design of paradox and irony. We become aware that this comedy involves us in an interplay between the conditioned, institutionalized morality of the law which the Duke thinks he wants at the play's inception, and the less admissible, less conditioned, more instinctive morality he accepts (with his final comment to Angelo) at the play's end. All the scenes leading up to Angelo's dis-

[8]*A Grammar of Motives* (New York, 1945), p. 514. I am indebted to Robert Tener for calling Burke's observation to my attention.

covery of his own liability to sexual desire, and to Isabella's discovery of her own contempt for her brother's wish to live at the expense of her saintliness, point to a disturbing and therefore interesting discrepancy between dogmatic virtue and a less rigid variety. R. W. Chambers has argued that the play turns on Christian mercy. I think it more accurate to say that the source of its hold over us is its slow revelation, reaching a climax in the scenes between Isabella and Angelo and between Isabella and Claudio, that a wholly satisfying evaluation of human actions goes beyond our ability to classify them according to categories of virtue fixed by theologians or by statutory law. Whether such actions be technically good or evil, technically legal or illegal, we are made aware that we truly evaluate them by the less conditioned, more nearly morally intuitive responses of that side of us which operates below the level of conscious dogma.

What disturbs us in this play is our almost inadmissible perception that below its neat, surface design of evil committed and evil caught out, *Measure for Measure* suggests evaluations of Angelo's and of Isabella's behavior which do not conform to the warm, well-lighted world of institutionalized good and evil we all wish to think we inhabit. *Measure for Measure,* both in its cumulative small scenes and in its climactic ones, carries with it the extra dimension of unstated but bold moral implication. It is enriched by the suggestive powers of the tone of its characters' response to the events of the play and to each other. We sense that underneath the neatly regimented ironies by which they are caught, Angelo and Isabella (like Hamlet and Ophelia) are created to appeal to our recognition of deep undercurrents in their motives and intentions. They have full power over us as dramatic creations *because* their motives and impulses are too rich to submit to easy identification with the surface virtues they profess and to which, chastened, they return. Their full power comes from our recognition of the fact that they are caught by the same haunting moral ambiguities we find lurking below the surface of our own behavior—and enriching it.

Chapter III

Measure for Measure and the Resistance of Its Critics

MEASURE FOR MEASURE seems always to have tempted certain of its critics to resist its full effect. An analysis of the nature of their resistance, and of those aspects of the play which have habitually provoked it, has a fascination in its own right to any serious admirer of the play. It has a special relevance for the twentieth century, however, because the adverse reactions of earlier critics, especially those of the nineteenth century, give perspective to the modern presumption that the effect of *Measure for Measure* is blurred by the nature of the play itself. Viewed in

historical perspective, this modern presumption seems to
be the result of a kind of intellectual inertia. We have
apparently been unable to let go entirely a romantic and
Victorian hostility to *Measure for Measure;* this hostility
has lingered on into the middle of our century, but cut
loose from the original reasons for it. We do not react
any longer, in nineteenth-century fashion, to the play's
lenient views of man in his sexual predicaments. But we
have substituted, instead, vaguely uneasy feelings that there
must be "something" unclear and strange at the heart of
the play.

The critical comment on *Measure for Measure* for the
first two decades in this century demonstrates this intellectual inertia, this reluctance to break completely with
Hazlitt's insistence that there is "an original sin in the
nature of the [play's] subject which prevents us from taking a cordial interest in it,"[1] and with Coleridge's view
that *Measure for Measure* is "a hateful work, although
Shakesperian throughout."[2] A. C. Bradley, as an example,
shows little eagerness to reconsider the nature of the play
and voices only the general reluctance of his time to go
much beyond an annoyed impatience with it. Thus he can
remark, tartly, that Shakespeare's marrying of Isabella to
the Duke is "a scandalous proceeding."[3] E. K. Chambers
disavows what he calls the nineteenth-century's "sentimental" rejection of *Measure for Measure,* but he is con-

[1]*Characters of Shakespeare's Plays,* in *The Complete Works of William Hazlitt,* ed. P. P. Howe (London and Toronto, 1931), IV, 345.

[2]*Selections from "Table Talk,"* in *Coleridge's Shakespearean Criticism,* ed. Thomas Middleton Raysor, 2 vols. (London, 1930), II, App. III, 352.

[3]*Shakespearean Tragedy* (London, 1905), p. 78.

tent to find in the play only "a particular phase in the poet's shifting outlook upon humanity," and a "nascent pessimism" which anticipates Shakespeare's writing of *King Lear*.[4] Brander Matthews casually links *Measure for Measure* with *All's Well* and *Troilus and Cressida* as plays "illmade on unworthy themes, carelessly thrown together."[5] And Odell, the Genest of the New York stage, a reliable spokesman for popular dramatic opinion and a man with few critical ideas about the aesthetics of drama, pairs *Measure for Measure* with *All's Well* as each having "a revolting plot," and happily consigns them both to "the stage oblivion into which they have fallen."[6]

It was Quiller-Couch who brought this malingering over *Measure for Measure* into sharp focus, in the introduction to his New Cambridge edition (1922), by asking point blank: "What is wrong with this play?" His question was quite legitimate because *Measure for Measure* had indeed fallen into a critical quagmire. He defended his question by asserting that all previous reaction to the play was tangled, confused, and contradictory, and that the play itself was not "pellucidly clear."[7] He cites as his evidence for this supposed tangle only the rather untangled remarks of Johnson, Coleridge, and Swinburne, though he does throw in a reference each to Gervinus and to Barrett Wendell for good measure. And his attempt to answer his own question came to rest, finally, on the inconsistency of Isabella as an exemplar of chastity—an inconsistency (as I have

[4]*Shakespeare: A Survey* (London, 1925), pp. 208–216.

[5]*Shakspere As a Playwright* (New York, 1913), pp. 220–221.

[6]*Shakespeare from Betterton to Irving*, 2 vols. (New York, 1920), II, 23.

[7]*Measure for Measure,* ed. Sir Arthur Quiller-Couch and John Dover Wilson, p. xiii.

noted in Chapter II) absolutely essential to the ameliorative tone of *Measure for Measure,* and built as an integral
and intended element into the basically ironic design of
the play.

The question posed by Quiller-Couch summed up this
early twentieth century hesitancy to re-examine the nature
of *Measure for Measure,* and gave the question a validity
for contemporary critics which it scarcely deserved. It is
this question, however, which has continued to haunt our
comment on *Measure for Measure.* Turned into a positive
assertion ("There *is* something wrong with this play"), it
is the phrase which has set in motion our eager and obses-
sive attempts to "explain" *Measure for Measure.* It has
brought into being both the view, initiated by W. W.
Lawrence, postulating one or another basic flaw in the
architecture of the play, and the view initiated by G.
Wilson Knight and R. W. Chambers that there is a recoverable religious meaning in the play. It is as much the
presupposition implicit in F. P. Wilson's comment that in
Measure for Measure Shakespeare "is finding some difficulty in putting the new wine of searching analysis of motives
into the old bottles of conventional story,"[8] as it is implicit
in Wylie Sypher's assertions concerning what he calls "the
structural instability of this comedy."[9]

Measure for Measure, to be sure, did in fact provoke a
nineteenth-century repudiation because of its conciliatory
suggestions concerning evil in the human condition. But
what Quiller-Couch's question fails to suggest, and what
contemporary criticism has often forgotten, is that there
was no mystery, no confusion, as to what was objected to

[8]*Elizabethan and Jacobean* (Oxford, 1945), p. 118.
[9]"Shakespeare as Casuist: *Measure for Measure,*" *Sewanee Review,*
LXVIII (1950), 271.

in the play until our own time. If one reads through the major comment on *Measure for Measure* written prior to the twentieth century, indeed, the nature of its critics' reactions is perfectly clear, and they find the *play* perfectly clear. Even in the Victorian era, *Measure for Measure* had one of its strongest admirers (and he was quite sure of what he admired in the play) in Walter Pater. Moreover, critics like Hazlitt, Coleridge, and Swinburne, whom *Measure for Measure* genuinely disturbed, though perhaps more vehement in their dislike than Pater in his admiration, still leave little doubt as to what it is in the play that disturbs them so much.

The continued resistance of our contemporary criticism to the full effect of *Measure for Measure,* and its limited enthusiasm for the play, seem to me extremely important to face directly. I take this resistance to be the peculiar one of a criticism being unable to withstand the momentum of its own search for answers to its own unnecessary unease with this play. Since Quiller-Couch's declaration of puzzlement, we have witnessed a proliferation of learned, often intellectually subtle, often highly speculative "explanations" of *Measure for Measure.* These explanations, however, have not really clarified the alleged difficulties in the play and made it more available to us. They have become, instead, a fascinating and substitute puzzle for the play in itself. We have produced nothing like agreement as to what the play is meant to signify as play, or as to whether it is an integrated, artistic whole. What we have achieved, I think, can best be described as two separate kinds of response to the question of the viability of *Measure for Measure* as drama. Each of the two has developed into a recognizable cult or school of criticism, moreover, where each new venture in analysis by a new recruit makes a further attempt to elaborate what has already been previously asserted by the older members of the group.

The first of these responses takes the view that whatever success *Measure for Measure* may once have had on the Jacobean stage, and interesting as it remains, it has failed to survive its own age as a wholly successful comedy. Those who hold this view[10] have created a body of criticism devoted to analyses of the degree and direction of the play's failure. The nature of its failure may be traced to peculiarities of early seventeenth-century taste in story materials which no longer act to give the play an essential probability. It may be traced to the play's inability to maintain a consistent tone, to an inconsistency in the characterization (especially of Isabella), or to a flaw in the dramatic structure. It may be traced to Shakespeare's personal moral and religious attitudes and prejudices, or to his private intellectual concerns when writing the play which, somehow, undermined his usual competence as a dramatist.

The second of the responses takes the view that *Measure for Measure* is unsuccessful only to those scholars and critics who are innocent of its original intentions. It can

[10]E.g., Quiller-Couch, already noted; W. W. Lawrence, in *Shakespeare's Problem Comedies* (New York, 1931); Oscar James Campbell, in *Shakespeare's Satire* (New York, 1943); Hardin Craig, in *An Interpretation of Shakespeare* (New York, 1948), and in *The Complete Works of Shakespeare* (New York, 1951), p. 834; E. M. W. Tillyard, in *Shakespeare's Problem Plays* (Toronto, 1949); Donald A. Stauffer, in *Shakespeare's World of Images* (New York, 1949). This older critical view lingers on. See Eileen Mackay's "Measure for Measure," *SQ,* XIV (1963), 109–113; Lawrence Sargent Hall's "Isabella's Angry Ape," *SQ,* XV (1964), 157–165; and Harold Skulsky's "Pain, Law, and Conscience in *Measure for Measure,*" *JHI,* XXV (1964), 147–168.

be demonstrated to have been an artistic whole in its own time if we take into consideration historical shifts in attitude, and correct our muddled twentieth-century response to Isabella, for example, by a consideration of the rigidity of Jacobean attitudes toward chastity in women.[11] A variant of this historical view, and the one given most credence by a host of modern commentators, is that *Measure for Measure* is a respository for theological symbolism. It can be considered a successful play, or at least an understandable one, by the reconstruction of its original, lost, and didactic meaning.[12] A critic's error in regarding Isabella as incon-

[11]The fullest argument concerning hypothetical Jacobean views of Isabella's chastity is in Elizabeth M. Pope's "The Renaissance Background of *Measure for Measure*," *Shakespeare Survey*, No. 2 (1949). John Wasson, in *"Measure for Measure: A* Play of Incontinence," *ELH* XXVII (1960), 262–275, argues that we should understand the forgiveness of Angelo, historically, by way of Aristotle: "I believe it can be shown that *Measure for Measure* reflects the entire discussion of continence and incontinence in Book VII of the *Ethics*" (p. 268). Three recent studies argue our need to consider the Renaissance concept of equity as a way of understanding the play: Skulsky's "Pain, Law, and Conscience;" John W. Dickinson, "Renaissance Equity and *Measure for Measure;*" *SQ*, XIII (1962), 287–297; Wilbur Dunkel, "Law and Equity in *Measure for Measure*," *SQ*, XIII (1962), 276–285.

[12]See G. Wilson Knight, *"Measure for Measure* and the Gospels," in *The Wheel of Fire* (London, 1930); R. W. Chambers, *Man's Unconquerable Mind* (London, 1939), Ch. IX; R. W. Battenhouse, *"Measure for Measure* and Christian Doctrine of Atonement," *PMLA*, LXI (1946); Francis Fergusson, "Philosophy and Theatre in *Measure for Measure*," *Kenyon Review*, XIV (1952), 103–120; Virgil K. Whitaker, *Shakespeare's Use of Learning* (San Marino, 1953), pp. 215–222; Nevill Coghill, "Comic Form in *Measure for Measure*," *Shakespeare Survey*, No. 8 (1955), pp. 14–27; J. A. Bryant, Jr., *Hippolyta's View* (Lexington, 1961), Ch. VI. Raymond Southall, in *"Measure for Measure* and the Protestant Ethic," *Essays in Criticism*,

sistent in her chastity can thus be corrected by a recreation
of the religious climate of opinion in which *Measure for
Measure* was written, and by a look at the play, and Isabella's role in it, through the eyes of a "normative" religious spectator of 1603–1604.

Both those contemporaries who insist upon discovering
reasons for the play's failure, and those who would save
the play from its detractors by means of historical or
historical-theological reconstruction, seem to be caught
with the illusion that the nature of *Measure for Measure*
is to be defined solely by the difficulties which as critics
they continue to insist that it contains. The first point of
view has created interesting scholarly speculation, but it is
a perilous basis for critical evaluation. It starts out with
our conventional assumption that *Measure for Measure*
is in some way ineffective, or defective, and then defends
this assumption with a variety of data extrinsic to the play.
But in considering the validity of Lawrence's thesis[13] that
a Jacobean taste for the improbabilities of traditional story
helps to explain the present-day limited success of the play,
one needs to note that such improbabilities are everywhere
endemic with Shakespeare. They no more convincingly
"explain" any hypothetical weakness in *Measure for Measure* than they "explain" the success of *Romeo and Juliet*
or of *Lear*. One would have to argue with the views of such
other members of this school as Hardin Craig, Tillyard,

XI (1961), 10–33, relates Angelo's forgiveness, and the ethical stance
of the play, historically, to the disintegration of medieval views of
Grace under the impact of Protestantism. But he defends the play
qua play: "In the distinctions made possible by involving ethical
material from the Grace controversy, Shakespeare deals with a conflict
and dilemma in human experience" (p. 20).

[13]See note 10 above.

and Stauffer,[14] moreover, that whether Shakespeare had a private wish to safeguard his heroine's chastity at the expense of the logic of the plot, or whether his usual skill as a dramatist was temporarily destroyed by muddled thinking about moral problems, are but guesses as to the content of Shakespeare's mind as he was writing the play. They may be tempting guesses to shore up an assumption of partial failure. But they seem something less than vivid insight into the play itself.

The views of the second group of critics, the historical or religious reconstructionists, seem to me to create the paradox that in order to save the play one must abandon it to a frame of reference which is itself remote from our time. The more such critics assert the need to recreate a moral-theological climate of opinion in which it "must have been written," the more they isolate it from the twentieth century, and the less viable it must become. The results of such labors, however modish, give us historicity and not a drama. If we really need instruction in substantial differences between Jacobean attitudes toward chastity or toward Christianity and our own today in order to understand *Measure for Measure,* then the play exists perforce in some middle ground of literature where it has a kind of endurance as a cultural document from the past, almost a museum piece. But it must relinquish the claims of its historical-religious critics to be a living entity, and a work of art, in our time.

One may concede to an uneasy criticism that *Measure for Measure* does strain away from any simple classification as comedy. It is too darkly ironic to fit our casual notions of what may be subsumed under the word "comedy." Its

[14]See note 10 above.

ironies of character and predicament do reach a final moment of balance in what is on its surface surely the most rational of Shakespeare's plays. But it is a moment unusually formal and arbitrary, one understandable only in terms of the unusual structure of the play. What I cannot concede to contemporary criticism is its prescriptive theory that the general purport of *Measure for Measure* is peculiarly illuminated by our knowledge of historical fact extrinsic to the design of the play, whereas that of *As You Like It* or of *Twelfth Night,* for example, is not. It is truly unbelievable that *Measure for Measure,* considered on the basis of its stage success alone, could have a special meaning in its own time, and one rediscoverable by ours, from which the historically or theologically uninitiated are peculiarly exempt.

When one moves backward in time to consider the nature of the adverse comment on *Measure for Measure* made by its seventeenth-, eighteenth-, and nineteenth-century critics, one finds very little that suggests our own concern with the play's faulty structuring, and nothing remotely like our concern with its possible theological implications. Dryden, writing about Shakespeare at about the distance we are today from Chekhov and Shaw, may perhaps be glancing adversely at the architecture of *Measure for Measure* when he describes the play as "so meanly written, that the Comedy neither caus'd your mirth, nor the serious part your concernment."[15] But if so, he robs his statement of all perceptive strength by applying it equally to *Winter's Tale* and to *Love's Labor's Lost.* Mrs.

---

[15]"Defence of the Epilogue. Or, An Essay on the Dramatique Poetry of the last Age," in *The Conquest of Granada* (London, 1672), p. 163.

Lennox, in 1753–1754, though almost wholly preoccupied with the moral implications of *Measure for Measure,* does venture the remark that Shakespeare "was resolved to torture it [his subject matter] into a Comedy," and that he introduced "improbable Incidents"[16] in order to bring about the denouement. And Samuel Johnson, in his edition of Shakespeare of 1765, seems to be glancing adversely at the balanced structuring of the play when he remarks that its "light or comick part is very natural and pleasing, but the graver scenes, if a few passages be excepted, have more labour than elegance. The plot is rather intricate than artful."[17]

Perhaps it was the popularity of *Measure for Measure* on the eighteenth-century stage (it ran in London for twenty-two out of thirty seasons during the years 1720–1750; and for twenty-four out of fifty seasons during the years 1750–1800), and the successes of Mrs. Cibber and Mrs. Siddons in the role of Isabella,[18] which combined to make almost wholly inadmissible the twentieth-century's theory that there may be something structurally defective in the play. By the nineteenth century, moreover, the critical reaction to its moral implications had reached sufficient intensity to make comment on mere structure seem an impertinence. Indeed, *Measure for Measure* almost vanished from the London stage after 1812, when Mrs.

[16]*Shakespear Illustrated...with Critical Remarks,* 3 vols. (London, 1753 and 1754), I, 28.

[17]*The Plays of William Shakespeare,* 8 vols. (London, 1765), I, 382.

[18]See John Genest, *Some Account of the English Stage from... 1660 to 1830,* 10 vols. (Bath, 1832); also Charles Beecher Hogan, *Shakespeare in the Theatre 1701–1800,* 2 vols. (Oxford, 1952 and 1957), I, 461, and II, 718.

Siddons retired.[19] Other than Swinburne's dislike for the ending of *Measure for Measure*,[20] a dislike arising from the play's moral implications, there is little nineteenth-century critical response to the play's mere dramatic design.

Prior to our age's running query as to what is wrong with the play, lay other obviously deeper, more pervasive resistances to the full import of *Measure for Measure*. They derive essentially from the fact (which we would feel too compromising to voice) that the play presents a thirsty sexuality in men and women, not from a dogmatically moral point of view, but from what we might now be tempted to describe as an "existential" one, one that exhibits this sexuality in the bright glare of its everyday reality. The play's teasing hint that one knock at one's own bosom to see what is there like Claudio, like Angelo, like Isabella, contained the power to provoke many of its eighteenth- and nineteenth-century commentators into irritated discourse. It was not discourse written in an effort to avoid the real nature of the play's implications (as with much contemporary criticism). It was, rather, an effort to face the implications built into *Measure for Measure* and to disagree, in outrage, with them.

The play's final moral view, then, was what primarily repulsed many commentators of the eighteenth and nine-

[19]It was performed in London for only six seasons in the nineteenth century, following Mrs. Siddon's retirement: at Covent Garden, 1815–1816; at Drury Lane 1823–1824 and 1828–1829; at Sadler's Wells in 1846; at the Haymarket in 1876 and 1878. There was a revival at the Adelphi Theatre, 1906. Its performance at Oxford in 1906 was protested by the town. (See Genest, and also Harold Child, "The Stage History," in the New Cambridge edition of *Measure for Measure,* pp. 160–165.)

[20]Algernon Charles Swinburne, *A Study of Shakespeare* (London, 1880), pp. 152–153 and pp. 202–205.

teenth centuries. Leavis has remarked of it that "if we don't see ourselves in Angelo, we have taken the play...very imperfectly." And he adds, in warning, that "if you can't accept what Shakespeare does provide, you have, in some way, to import your interest and significance."[21] Critics as varied as Johnson, Coleridge, and Swinburne seem to have taken the play perfectly, yet have boldly rejected both Angelo and the moral insight which his reinstatement *does* provide. In our own time, and after Quiller-Couch, many critics, however, have simply shied away from confronting the fundamental intentions of *Measure for Measure*. It is they who have taken the second course and and have gone *outside* the play to import extrinsic explanations for it.

The adverse criticism of *Measure for Measure* written before our century which takes clear exception to the moral commitments of the play focuses its pejorative attention primarily on the forgiveness of Angelo and the restitution of his good name. Two other important aspects of the play have also provoked the ire of early critics: its blunt, pervasive sex-talk, especially as bawdily voiced by Lucio, Pompey, Elbow, and Mistress Overdone; and the characterization of Isabella whereby female innocence and purity is made to appear in the guise of a heartless shrew. No one critic is necessarily antagonistic to all three aspects of *Measure for Measure*. Johnson, for example, objected strenuously to the play's forgiveness of Angelo, praised Lucio and the bawdy, comic thread of the play, and regarded Isabella somewhat equivocally. But the generally harsh tones in which eighteenth- and nineteenth-century critics resisted *Measure for Measure* on any one of these three points suggests the insistent strength of Shakespeare's play, its

---

[21]"The Greatness of *Measure for Measure*," in *The Importance of Scrutiny*, ed. Eric Bentley (New York, 1948), pp. 161–162.

ability to provoke reaction, to penetrate below the surface into the private emotional domain of the individual critic.

In attempting to account for the vehement reactions of Johnson and other lesser critics to Angelo's reconciliation with his world, it is important to observe that Shakespeare himself deliberately altered the basic story of the monstrous ransom as radically as he was to alter the ending to the legendary story of King Lear. (And one might recall, in this connection, A. C. Bradley's feeling that the original Lear story was perhaps right in having a different, and happy, ending.) The basic story, as found in Thomas Lupton's *Siuquila* (1580–1581), in Belleforest's *Histoires Tragiques* (1583), in Edward Grimestone's translation of Simon Goulart's *Histoires* (1607), and as late as Steele's retelling of the story in *The Spectator* (1712, No. 491), makes the condemned man (the ur-Claudio) the husband, not the brother, of the woman who pleads for him. It is the wife (the ur-Isabella) who fulfills the sexual terms of her husband's ransom. The husband is then immediately executed, and higher authority steps in, marries the wife to seducer-judge, and then executes the judge. As Mary Lascelles carefully sums up her analysis of this archetype, "the theme remains constant: a representation of wrong-doing and retribution, of power exerted to the utmost against weakness, and weakness at last gathering itself up to appeal beyond power to authority."[22] And in its original versions, this story always ends, as the Duke put it bluntly, with its Angelo executed for executing its Claudio, with "death for death," and "measure for measure." It is the kind of tale, as Steele saw it, in which an audience can fully and happily relish "revenge for the offense done."

Geraldi Cinthio was the first person to tamper with the

[22]*Shakespeare's "Measure for Measure"* (London, 1953), p. 7.

simple outlines of this tale of the monstrous ransom, and thereby to alter and to complicate its moral significance. His first version, published in his *Hecatommithi* (1565) transforms the husband-wife of the original into the more complex emotional situation of brother-sister, intensifies the brother's guilt by turning his sexual crime into rape, executes the brother, but has the sister forgive the brother's guilty judge and marry him. Cinthio's second version of this theme, found in his play published in 1583, goes one step further in complicating the story. It saves both the brother and his judge by having another man executed in the brother's stead. In essentials, this is the new version used by Whetstone in his *Promos and Cassandra,* Shakespeare's immediate source for *Measure for Measure.*

Shakespeare's sense of the deeper possibilities for this story not only led him to accept the plot of the Cinthio-Whetstone revision. It also led him to make central the role of the Duke (the character merely representing "higher authority" in the original story) and to create a sister-victim, interesting dramatically by virtue of her conventual status. Further, it led him to insist upon the forgivable nature of both the judge's lust for his victim and for his abortive attempt to execute his victim's brother. Shakespeare's version, finally, insists upon stepping up the complexity of the Cinthio-Whetstone story by presenting evil intents which turn out to be, as Isabella says, "merely thoughts," not acts, and by arguing the concept of the vileness of the fault, but the pardonable act of the man who commits it (II.ii.35). It is amazing how many eighteenth- and nineteenth-century critics rejected outright Shakespeare's alterations and insight out of a preference for the "simple" pleasures Steele had derived from the eye-for-an-eye justice of the basic story.

Among the earlier critics who have been tempted to resist the full impact of Shakespeare's own version of the monstrous ransom, there is a fair amount of variation in the language used, as well as in the degree of irritation behind it. Mrs. Lennox, at about the middle of the eighteenth century, wished for "one good Beheading" at the end of the play as "the Consequence naturally expected."[23] Mrs. Inchbald, half a century later, argued that Angelo as conceived in Shakespeare's *Measure for Measure,* was nothing less than a pure monster. She wished that he had been allowed to recognize Mariana during the assignation so that his attempted killing of Claudio would appear to the audience as revenge for Isabella's cheating him. She concluded that if Angelo had been created by Shakespeare as "less wicked, he would be hated more."[24] But it was Johnson who gave classic expression to the view that Shakespeare had violated some fundamental moral propriety, some basic moral perception, in his treatment of Angelo. Johnson pleads against Isabella's views and those of the Duke (and the play's) that Angelo "had committed all the crimes charged against him, as far as he could commit them." And he concludes: "Angelo's crimes were such, as must sufficiently justify punishment, whether its end be to secure the innocent from wrong, or to deter the guilty by example; and I believe every reader feels some indignation when he finds him spared."[25] Such Romantic and Victorian critics as Coleridge and Swinburne merely repeated Johnson's castigations with an equal vehemence, and in their own style.

[23]*Shakespear Illustrated,* I, 28.
[24]"Remarks," in *The British Theatre* (London, 1808), III, 4.
[25]*The Plays of William Shakespeare,* I, 377–378, note 6 to V. vii.

The second of the aspects of *Measure for Measure* which have provoked a moralistic attack on the play, the common denominator of sex as it is given bawdy and comic expression by Lucio and company, is a sort of minor corollary to the critics' major concern over Angelo's forgiveness. Adverse reactions to this element are pretty much confined to the second half of the eighteenth century where they are a matter of taste, and to the whole of the nineteenth century, where they are a matter of prudery. We see the reaction of the eighteenth century, most directly, in the alterations and excisions in the text first of Younger's Covent Garden acting version published in 1774, and then in Kemble's Drury Lane version (as used by Mrs. Siddons) published in 1803. In both texts one finds much refinement of vocabulary. Typical of Younger's and of Kemble's revisions is the substitution of "wenching" for "lechery" in the exchange between Claudio and Lucio in I.ii. Elbow, Froth, and Pompey are removed entirely from II.i. in both texts, and Younger notes as his reason that the scene is "too full of indecencies." In III.ii Lucio's gross references to the begetting of Angelo, to Claudio's "rebellion of a codpiece," etc., are either cut entirely from both texts, or given some kind of paraphrase. Again, Younger notes that the whole scene ought to be dropped as "low ribaldry...too indecent to bear."[26] The main effect of Younger's and of Kemble's attempts to refine Lucio and his fellows, however, was to rob their language of its penetrating power, and thus to weaken somewhat the impact of the play.

In the nineteenth century, the bawdy comic element of *Measure for Measure* was an easy target for the puritan in editor and in critic. Harness, for example, speaks of the

[26]*Bell's Shakespeare* (London, 1774), *Measure for Measure*, III, 283 ff.

"repulsive levity of the votaries of licentiousness" in *Measure for Measure*.[27] Wheeler refers to the "digusting ribaldry...exhibited in this piece."[28] Knight comments, adversely, that there is "an atmosphere of impurity hanging like a dense fog over the city of the poet."[29] Earlier than these editorial denigrations is Mrs. Inchbald's annoyed reaction: "That Dr. Johnson, in his criticism on this play, should write in praise of the comick characters, seems surprising!"[30] And Coleridge, in his marginal notes to his Theobald edition of Shakespeare (1773), rejects the comic part of the play by the word "digusting."[31] Odell's early twentieth-century reference to the "Overdone-Froth-Elbow-Pompey nastiness"[32] in *Measure for Measure* represents a late echo of this nineteenth-century prudery.

The third aspect of *Measure for Measure* excoriated by critics is the play's characterization of Isabella (especially in Act III) as a woman who is merciless when her own image of herself as an exemplar of chastity is touched. This characterization is the most venerable object of attack in this play, that by virtue of it, innocence and purity have been dramatized as wearing the disguise of shrewishness and vindictiveness. Moreover, it is this one objection which has not been cut off but has rather been intensified by Quiller-Couch's questioning of the play. It extends in time from D'Avenant's rewriting and "softening" the part of

[27]*The Dramatic Works,* 8 vols. (London, 1825), II, 167, note to V.i.

[28]*The Dramatic Works* (London, 1827), p. 814.

[29]*The Pictorial Edition of the Works of Shakespeare,* 8 vols. (London, ed. 1864), II, 328.

[30]*The British Theatre,* III, 5.

[31]Notes on title page of Vol. I following p. 303; in British Museum. Printed in *Coleridge's Shakespearean Criticism,* ed. T. M. Raysor, 2 vols. (London, 1930), I, 113–114.

[32]*Shakespeare from Betterton to Irving,* II, 60.

Isabella in his late seventeenth-century version of *Measure for Measure,* and from Mrs. Lennox's vituperations against Isabella as a "vixen," in the eighteenth century, down to Dame Edith Sitwell's previously noted comment, in the twentieth, that Isabella is "cold and repellent," and an "unconscious hypocrite."[33]

The attack on Isabella centers most often on the violence with which she rejects Claudio's plea that she intercede for his life by paying the monstrous ransom demanded by Angelo. But the moral ease with which she is willing to let Mariana intercede in her brother's behalf is also often deplored. Here and there, moreover, a very alert critic has found her identification of Claudio with her father when he agrees with her, and with a mother probably unfaithful to her husband when Claudio disagrees, also wholly objectionable. And curiously, as with the play's forgiveness of Angelo and its inclusion of Lucio's rich vein of bawdy talk, so with Isabella's characterization. Much of the early adverse criticism, often by implication only, seems mere irritation, or sometimes even a kind of equivocal admiration. It does not take the part for the whole and move adversely against the whole play.

Charlotte Lennox and Samuel Johnson were the most articulate of the eighteenth-century critics of Isabella, and their remarks pretty much set the pattern for a reaction which has persisted down to the present time. Mrs. Lennox, the more vehement of the two, describes Isabella as "a mere Vixen in her Virtue," and feels that she might have been expected to meet Claudio's "Desire of Life" which was "a natural Frailty" with "mild Expostulations, wise Reasonings, and gentle Rebukes." Instead we get "those

[33]*A Poet's Notebook* (Boston, 1950), pp. 122–123, 128.

coarse and unwomanly Reflexions on the Virtue of her Mother" and "her exulting Cruelty to the dying Youth." She concludes that Isabella is no "pious innocent and tender Maid," but a woman with "the manners of an affected Prude, outragious in her Seeming Virtue."[34] Johnson reacted somewhat less strenuously toward the Isabella of the first half of the play, noting of her wild and whirling words to Claudio only that in them "there is something harsh, and something forced and far-fetched. But her indignation cannot be thought violent when we consider her not only as a virgin but as a nun." It was the Isabella of the second half, pleading for her betrayer Angelo, that truly disturbed Johnson, and led to his famous indictment of both Isabella and of Shakespeare: "I am afraid our Varlet Poet intended to inculcate, that women think ill of nothing that raises the credit of their beauty, and are ready, however virtuous, to pardon any act which they think incited by their own charms."[35]

Typical of nineteenth-century adverse comments on Isabella are those of Coleridge that "Isabella herself contrives to be unamiable,"[36] and that of Hazlitt that he is not "greatly enamoured of Isabella's rigid chastity," and that he lacks "confidence in the virtue that is 'sublimely good' at another's expense."[37] Horne, in his notes to White's edition of the plays (1857–1859), is much more explicit, and approaches Mrs. Lennox in harshness of tone. He finds Isabella "energetically virtuous," a woman who lays "deliberate plans to preserve a continence... she need apprehend

---

[34]*Shakespear Illustrated,* I, 32–34.

[35]*The Plays of William Shakespeare,* I, 321, note 5; 377–378, note 6.

[36]In Raysor, *Coleridge's Shakespearean Criticism,* II, 352.

[37]*The Complete Works of William Hazlitt,* ed. P. P. Howe (London and Toronto, 1931), IV, 346.

no temptation to relax." To Horne, she is "a pietist in her religion, a pedant in her talk, a prude in her notions, a prig in her conduct."[38] When one comes to the condemnations of Isabella by twentieth-century critics, the most important one is that of Quiller-Couch, already referred to, that she was inconsistent in her chastity.

What is central to all the adverse views of Isabella, from those of eighteenth-century critics to those of the present, is that they express in a negative and derogatory fashion the more nearly neutral essence of her actual role. One might say that a partial "not-liking" of Isabella is written into the play, at least into its first half. Whether it is Oxberry, in 1822, writing acidly that Isabella "has our respect ...extracted...as a duty,"[39] or Ridley, in 1937, who notes that Isabella abuses Claudio "from an unnecessary pulpit,"[40] the comment reflects the deliberate ambiguity of her role in the play. Isabella's invective sits uneasily with most of us, even as we realize that it is a principal source of our interest in her. Yet why we should wish, or expect, an inhuman consistency in Isabella has not yet been revealed to us by Quiller-Couch, or by Isabella's other detractors. It is her mimetic closeness to reality that makes her at once fascinating to us, and arouses our resentment. We both "understand" and are annoyed by the verisimilitude of her behavior to that found in the everyday reality outside the theatre—as the play no doubt intends.

I do not wish this long discussion of a three-faced histor-

[38]*Complete Works,* ed. R. G. White and R. H. Horne, 3 vols. (London, 1857–1859), I, 593.

[39]*Measure for Measure, with Prefatory Remarks* (London, 1822), p. iv.

[40]*Shakespeare's Plays, A Commentary* (London, 1937), p. 145

ical hostility to imply that *Measure for Measure* has always been resisted. On the contrary, appreciative reaction to the play flourished cheerfully alongside the derogatory comment of the eighteenth century and occasionally alongside that of the nineteenth century. Moreover, and understandably, those critics who have voiced a liking for *Measure for Measure* prior to our era have tended to single out for special comment and pleasure (creating a kind of mirror image of the adverse criticism), precisely the three aspects which have aroused so much hostility: the merciful ending of the play with the readmission of Angelo to society, the lively undercurrents of sex-talk in Lucio and his companions, and Isabella's thorny chastity. In comparing the paired negative and positive critical reactions to *Measure for Measure,* indeed, one is forced to face up to the fact that a basic element in its power over us is precisely that it contains so rich an assortment of built-in moral ambivalences and paradoxes.

A rather generalized liking for the lenient concept of justice in *Measure for Measure* really begins with the play's first critic, Charles Gildon, in his *Remarks on the Plays of Shakespear,* published in 1710 as a seventh volume appended to Rowe's edition of the plays of 1709. He reacts in simple pleasure to the formal denouement. He thinks it, "allowing for some Peccadillos," to be "wonderful, and moving to such a Degree, that he must have very little Sense of Things, and Nature, who finds himself Calm in the reading it." He does not comment directly on the forgiveness of Angelo, but notes indirectly (somewhat in Lucio's fashion) that the "Design of the Play carries an excellent Moral, and a just Satire against our present Reformers; who wou'd alter their Course of Nature, and bring us to a Perfection, Mankind never knew since the World was half peopled."[41]

Other eighteenth-century critics, subsequent to Gildon, who accepted the Duke's final distribution of sympathy and acceptance, tended to be more general in their remarks than were Mrs. Lennox or Samuel Johnson in their joint disapproval. Theobald, for instance (1733), glances at the mood of the play's Act V when he notes that "the Pardon of Barnardine, gives a fine Opportunity of making the Duke's Character more amiable both for Mercy, and Virtue."[42] The critic for *The London Chronicle* (1757), in a review of one of Mrs. Cibber's last performances as Isabella, summed up Shakespeare's special version of the monstrous ransom with the comment that the "Story of this Piece is extremely affecting and interesting."[43] The editorial commentator in Bell's Covent Garden acting version (1774) is a bit more specific. He glances at Charlotte Lennox's outraged cry that *"Measure for Measure* ought not to be the Title, since Justice is not the Virtue it inculcates,"[44] and notes that "the Title of the play to persons not very intelligent, sounds rather odd, but the play fully justifies and appropriates it." He finds that the Duke's rebuff of Isabella, in Act V, renders "Angelo's situation more interesting." And he concludes that the Duke's disposition of affairs is "strictly just" and "exceedingly pleasing."[45]

[41](London, 1710), pp. 293, 342.

[42]*The Works of Shakespeare: in Seven Volumes* (London, 1733), I, 396, note 30.

[43]Vol. I, "The Theatre," No. 18 (March 1, 1757), p. 215.

[44]*Shakespear Illustrated,* I, 37.

[45]Younger, in *Bell's Shakespeare,* III, 285, note; 377, note; 348, note.

In the nineteenth century one gets a similar scattering of rather general comment approving the moral direction of the play, in such remarks as Hudson's (1872) that *Measure for Measure* "is the deepest of Shakespeare's comedies," and that in it "the foundation principles of ethics are... explored far as the plummet of thought can sound."[46] It was Pater, however, who really put into words the opposite point of view from that of Johnson and Coleridge toward the moral atmosphere of Act V. He described the kind of justice caught by *Measure for Measure* as "a finer knowledge through love."[47] John Masefield, writing in 1911, is suggesting much the same thing in his remark that in *Measure for Measure* "Shakespeare seems to have brooded on the fact that the common prudential virtues are sometimes due, not to virtue, but to some starvation of the nature."[48]

As far as the common denominator of sex in *Measure for Measure* is concerned, it seems always to have been understood and approved except in late eighteenth-century acting versions, and in a prudish recoil from it observable in some nineteenth-century comment. Wherever one touches upon admiration for Lucio, Elbow, Pompey, and Mistress Overdone, from Gildon to the present, the remarks are very much alike. Gildon liked the naturalness "of the Bawd and the Pimp; as well as of Lucio, which Character is admirably maintained."[49] The critic of *The London*

[46]H. N. Hudson, *Shakespeare: His Life, Art, and Characters,* 2 vols. (Boston, ed. 1891), I, 398.

[47]"Appreciations," *The Works of Walter Pater,* 8 vols. (London, 1901), V, 183–184.

[48]*William Shakespeare (Home University Library of Modern Knowledge* [London, 1911]), p. 175.

[49]*Remarks on the Plays of Shakespear,* p. 292.

Chronicle of 1758 noted that "both for humour and nature" Lucio was "by many degrees superior to any character of the same stamp, introduced upon the stage since."[50] Johnson I have already cited for his thinking "the light or comick part" to be "very natural and pleasing." And one might add that he also felt that "after the pardon of two murderers, Lucio might be treated by the good Duke with less harshness."[51] Despite his cutting the role back, Younger as commentator in the Bell acting version (1774) noted that the part of Lucio was "more in favour of the actor, than any other in the piece."[52] Oxberry, in his notes to his acting version of 1822, found "the comic portions are invariably excellent."[53] Hazlitt, in 1817, thought Lucio, Pompey, and Master Froth pleasant persons and ones "comfortable in their occupations."[54] In our own time, Goddard in 1951, and W. W. Lawrence in 1958, have summarized about 250 years of pleasure in Lucio and company. As Goddard puts it, "we are more in love in the end with the disreputable than with the reputable characters. Overworld and underworld threaten to change places."[55] W. W. Lawrence remarks that Lucio "has the saving grace of a ready wit at the moment of disaster." For this reason "we love him, as we love Falstaff."[56]

[50]Vol. IV, "Postscript, The Theatre," p. 367.

[51]*The Plays* (1765), I, 380, note 1.

[52]*Bell's Shakespeare*, III, 292, note.

[53]*Measure for Measure*, p. vi.

[54]*The Complete Works*, IV, 348, notes.

[55]Harold C. Goodard, *The Meaning of Shakespeare* (Chicago, 1951), p. 450.

[56]"*Measure for Measure* and Lucio", *SQ*, IX (1958). See also Northrop Frye, "Characterization in Shakespearian Comedy," *SQ*, IV (1953), 276–277.

When we confront the many admirers of Isabella as a model of cloistered purity in the naughty world of the play, we find that they are all as blind to the ambiguities of her character as are those who excoriate her. The wholly admiring comment on Isabella's moral sternness begins, I think, in the late eighteenth-century's reactions to Mrs. Siddon's creation of the role. According to Thomas Campbell, in his *Life of Mrs. Siddons* (1834), she played the role "to inspire us with an exulting sympathy with Isabella."[57] In evaluating her Isabella, it is therefore necessary to observe the liberties which the Kemble acting version took with the text. Most of the low comedy is cut away. Almost all of Angelo's references to sex are dropped, as are Isabella's harsh references to her mother's infidelity. Moreover, a ten-line, sentimental epilogue is added, underlining the Duke's romantic attachment to Isabella. The Kemble version actually creates a much softer, more amiable Isabella than Shakespeare's play would allow. But Mrs. Siddons, no doubt, was more concerned with her rights to a sympathetic part than with the mere integrity of the views of Shakespeare's play.

It is the nineteenth-century editor or critic, however, who voiced the happiest cries of exultation that Isabella preferred her brother dead to the loss of her chastity. Harness, in 1825, regarded Claudio "as an object of disgust." He contrasted "the holy chastity of Isabella" with the "repulsive levity of the votaries of licentiousness."[58] To Singer, in 1826, Isabella is "a lovely example of female purity and virtue"[59]—especially when she is denouncing

[57] In 2 vols. (London, 1834), I, 200.
[58] *The Dramatic Works,* II, 167.
[59] *The Dramatic Works,* 10 vols., ed. Samuel Weller Singer (Chiswick, 1826), II, 3.

Claudio. Bowdler, as one would expect, felt that Isabella's reaction to Claudio's plea for life permitted the reader to overlook the "many great defects"[60] of the comedy. Mrs. Anna Murphy Jameson, in 1832, as everyone knows, admired Isabella for her "moral grandeur, a saintly grace, something of vestal dignity and purity."[61] Hudson, in 1851, felt that Isabella's "harshness does her honour."[62] And Dowden, to sum up the nineteenth century, finds Isabella to have a "white passion of purity and of indignation against sin."[63]

Few critics in the twentieth century have been able to regard Isabella with such simple fervor, though Peter Alexander, in a witty reaction to moral castigations of Isabella, has remarked of her angry critics that "the charity of Shakespeare's art embraces the virtuous as well as the sinner."[64] The real problem, of course, in dealing with Isabella (as also with the Duke and with Lucio) is to consider how she functions as a character in a play. But much of the post–Quiller-Couch criticism of her role seems to have merely created new and unnecessarily complicated views of her. When she is defended by such historical critics as Miss Pope, it is by advancing the concept of a Jacobean audience (more prone than we are to value chastity over mercy) actually enjoying the spectacle of Isabella's denunciation of Claudio. And Isabella, as we are now all aware, is regarded by the newly fashionable exponents of a Christian exegesis of the play as a kind of Christ figure in an

[60]*The Family Shakspeare* (London, 1831), p. 86.

[61]*Characteristics of Women,* 2 vols. (London, 1832), I, 43.

[62]*The Works,* 11 vols. (Boston, 1851), II, 13.

[63]*Shakspere: A Critical Study of his Mind and Art* (London, 1875), p. 125.

[64]*Shakespeare's Life and Art* (London, 1939), p. 191.

allegory or a parable, putting behind her the worldly considerations of the Devil Angelo (and his disciple Claudio).

I would view the sheer quantity both of invective and of praise directed toward Isabella for the past two centuries as a tribute to the skill with which she was created rather than as a battle to be won for either point of view. Her characterization as a woman with a dual role in the play is the source of her great dramatic interest. It is neither romantic nor wholly pleasant to contemplate innocence and chastity speaking with Isabella's strident voice up to the middle of *Measure for Measure*. But it is gratifying to find innocence and chastity almost voicelessly at work, as they are in the Isabella of the second half of the play. And if we are, in some sense of the phrase, all children of Adam, as *Measure for Measure* surely assumes, why should we wish or expect the play to celebrate a less ambiguous Isabella than Shakespeare gives us? I will give the final word on this ambiguity in her character to F. R. Leavis: "It is surely significant that the play should end upon a hint that she is to marry the Duke—a hint that, implying a high valuation along with a criticism, aptly clinches the general presentment of her."[65]

In summary, one needs perhaps to reiterate the fact that *Measure for Measure* has tempted earlier critics as diverse as Johnson and Coleridge to object to its moral views, and as diverse as Gildon and Pater to defend it because of its moral views. But this fact does not make the criticism of *Measure for Measure* a tangle of contradictions, nor imply some mysterious "wrongness" in the play. To the contrary, the eighteenth- and nineteenth-century critics

[65]"The Greatness of *Measure for Measure*," p. 158.

simply take sides concerning the highly individualized concept of justice, the rich vein of bawdy, the harsh tone of
the heroine's discourse, in Shakespeare's dramatized version
of the ubiquitous story of the monstrous ransom. A critic
like Johnson, with a strong feeling for institutionalized
morality, and a critic like Pater, with an equally strong
feeling for a morality "based on a more delicate appreciation of the true conditions of men and things,"[66] tend to
be provoked into comment on *Measure for Measure* in
opposite ways. But both critics would have agreed that
they were talking about the same play, and that the play
was not obscure.

Samuel Johnson's remark that "there is perhaps not one
of Shakespeare's plays more darkened than this by the
peculiarities of its Authour",[67] indeed suggests that his
adverse criticism of *Measure for Measure* is not a rejection
of the play itself. It is rather his statement for the record
of attitudes and commitments in the play which irritated
him. Likewise, Coleridge's comment (noted at the beginning of this chapter) that *Measure for Measure* "is a hateful
work, although Shakespearian throughout," suggests the
critic's unhappy awareness of the play's powerful implications, and is a kind of admission of its insistent strength.

One needs to observe, however, that there has been an
absolute change in attitude toward *Measure for Measure*
in our contemporary criticism of the play. It has remained
for our time to tempt itself with the notion of reacting to
something inexplicable in *Measure for Measure*. This stubborn and tempting "something" has been held to be an odd
defect in the structure of the play. It has recently been
more popular to regard it as a recoverable Jacobean atti-

[66]"Appreciations," *The Works*, V, 183–184.
[67]*The Plays* (1765), I, 263.

tude or a cluster of attitudes toward chastity in women, or as a recoverable Jacobean awareness of religious symbolism or parable in the play. But either way, it is part of a seething contemporary interest in importing into *Measure for Measure* meanings unguessed by at least two centuries of previous criticism.

Chapter IV

Measure for Measure and Theological Exegesis

TWENTIETH-CENTURY interpreters of *Measure for Measure* have proposed to rescue the play from a charge of obscurity by relocating its power to excite our sensibilities in its hitherto unremarked Christian implications and meanings. Their view takes its place beside such current interpretations of Shakespeare as that the tragic import, for the Jacobean audience at least, of Othello's killing both Desdemona and himself was that he went straight to the Christian torments of hell once the play was over.[1] It joins

[1] See Paul N. Siegel, "The Damnation of Othello," *PMLA,* LXVIII (1953), 1068–1078; and LXXI (1956), 279–280; and Roland M. Frye, "The Accepted Ethics and Theology of Shakespeare's Audience," *Dissertation Abstracts,* XV, 581–582 (1952).

forces with a new insight which finds that Hamlet, for all the flurry over the cause of his melancholy by Polonius, Claudius, T. S. Eliot, and Dr. Ernest Jones, would have been looked at by a normal Elizabethan Christian simply as God's inadequate scourge and minister;[2] and that Romeo and Juliet, far from being merely the embodiment of fragile, youthful passion, as some centuries of audiences have thought, take on fresh significance when they are demonstrated to be part of an Elizabethan sense of "human degeneration."[3]

Virgil Whitaker, in his biographical-analytical study, *Shakespeare's Use of Learning,* asserts this current religious view of Shakespeare's comic and tragic art with admirable boldness. Shakespeare as a man of the Renaissance, he assures us, had accepted the basic religious training of his youth and had never experienced "a genuine skepticism." It follows from such a premise that Shakespeare "did believe profoundly that God had made man in His own image and that, as all men had fallen once in Adam, so each man might fall again if he disobeyed the fundamental laws of God."[4] Whitaker, when he turns to aesthetics, is therefore led to argue, for example, that "Macbeth's sin is so awful simply because, like Shakespeare, he knows and believes in the foundations of human morality and in their ultimate basis in the mind and will of God."[5] This is no

[2]See Fredson Bowers, "Hamlet as Minister and Scourge," *PMLA,* LXX (1955), 740–749; and Sister Miriam Joseph, "*Hamlet,* A Christian Tragedy," *Studies in Philology,* LIX, No. 2, pt. I (1962), 119–140.

[3]Roland M. Frye, p. 582. See also Franklin M. Dickey, *Not Wisely But Too Well* (San Marino, 1957), p. 117.

[4](San Marino, 1953), p. 42.

[5]Page 42.

doubt to praise Shakespeare and Macbeth as sternly religious men, rather than as superlative playwright and brilliantly conceived character. Moreover, the implications seem to be that the sternness of the religion begot the strength of the play. And some such assumption of a highly self-conscious, febrile religious orthodoxy, both in Shakespeare and in his audience, seems to underlie the critical comments on Shakespeare by the whole contemporary school of Christian aesthetics.

One might suggest, if one wished to pursue the biographical fallacy through *Macbeth* as valid criticism of the play, that Santayana used this same tragedy to make an equally strong case for Shakespeare as almost wholly non-theological and a-theistic in his point of view.[6] A. C. Bradley long ago concluded (wisely), that Shakespeare "confined his view to the world of non-theological observation and thought."[7]

Robert Stevenson, in *Shakespeare's Religious Frontier* (1958), has simply denied outright Whitaker's point of view by referring to lines and to scenes from the plays as his clear evidence. And Roland M. Frye, in his recent study *Shakespeare and Christian Doctrine* (1963), argues from a sophisticated knowledge of Luther, Calvin, and Hooker, "theologians who in different ways epitomize the major religious attitudes of Shakespeare's culture,"[8] that much

[6]"The Absence of Religion in Shakespeare," in *Interpretations of Poetry and Religion* (New York, 1957), p. 155. See also George Santayana, "Tragic Philosophy" (1936), in *The Importance of Scrutiny,* ed. Eric Bentley (New York, 1948), pp. 203–213.

[7]*Shakespearean Tragedy* (London, 1904 and 1932), p. 25.

[8](Princeton), p. 14. In Ch. I, "Theologizing Analyses: The School of Knight," Frye challenges the validity of the theological views of the Renaissance as proposed by G. Wilson Knight, Paul N. Siegel, Irving Ribner, J. A. Bryant, Jr., and Roy W. Battenhouse.

current Christian exegesis of Shakespeare goes astray because its practitioners are ignorant of, or neglect, the views of these men.

The significant question in attempting to present the full effect of *Measure for Measure,* however, is not whether a given theological interpretation of the play is wholly accurate in its use of the attitudes of Luther, Calvin, or Hooker. It is rather a question as to whether a theological-historical "reconstruction" of *Measure for Measure* is genuinely valid as literary criticism. Is this play so very different from the other comedies that it cannot be fully comprehended if treated as a self-contained dramatic entity? Is it possible, one asks, that some rather specific (and hopefully correct) Jacobean-Christian frame of reference *must* be found for *Measure for Measure* so that we can at least come to terms with its form and substance?

Is it remotely possible, as Roy W. Battenhouse has maintained, that "the pattern of presuppositions in terms of which the play can be made ultimately intelligible"[9] *is* basically a Christian one, or, as he analyzes it more narrowly, the doctrine of the Atonement? If so, we must assume (which seems very difficult to do) that the early seventeenth-century audiences which witnessed *Measure for Measure* were unusually doctrinaire, and zealously alert and eager for specific Christian reference in popular drama. But more importantly, we must also assume that all the secular critical comment on *Measure for Measure* which has found the play understandable, from that of Charles Gildon in the early eighteenth century to that of the twentieth-century F. R. Leavis, must be abandoned as quite imperceptive [which it obviously is not], and that the play has

[9]"*Measure for Measure* and Christian Doctrine of Atonement," *PMLA,* LXI (1946), 1032.

remained relatively unintelligible from its own day until our neotheologians made all clear [which they have not].

Christian apologists who would explain the success of *Measure for Measure* by theological or by quasi-theological interpretations have focussed their attention (pretty much in the pattern set by the nontheological critics of the eighteenth and nineteenth centuries) both on Isabella's reaction to her brother's plea for life and on the ameliorative tone of the final Act V. But they generally part company with earlier and contemporary secular critics, from Mrs. Charlotte Lennox to Dame Edith Sitwell, by venturing the assertion, sometimes with a sprinkling of historical data, sometimes by personal fiat, that Jacobeans might well have considered Isabella's wishing her brother dead a proper Christian position to take and one that we also might take to further comprehend the play. They also part company with Johnson and Coleridge, who preferred the original "lex talionis" ending of the Renaissance story of the monstrous ransom, by regarding the all-round forgiveness of Act V of *Measure for Measure* as literally and intentionally analogous to Christ's forgiveness of all men who fell in Adam.

The most dispassionate attempt to reconstruct hypothetical "Christian" reactions of an early Jacobean audience to Isabella's stubborn chastity is to be found in Elizabeth M. Pope's article "The Renaissance Background of *Measure for Measure*." But it is not, for me at least, wholly convincing as to the intent of the scene in which Isabella turns on her brother. She cites (from Luke vi, 38: Geneva Version, London, 1599) the summarizing, key passage from Christ's Sermon on the Mount concerning rendering judgment and mercy: "for with what measure ye mete, with the same shall men mete to you again." She refers to a series of Renaissance comments on the limitations imposed by this passage as it might apply to private behavior. She concludes that the very restrictions set by Jacobean theological commentators on the possibilities of Christian mercy in daily life suggest that they, and therefore Shakespeare's audience, would have approved Isabella's excoriations of Claudio:

> When...we remember the limitations which Renaissance doctrine set on both charity and forbearance, we have no right to assume that Shakespeare is deliberately and cynically implying that his heroine is, in her own way, as narrow and cold as his villain. He seems rather to be trying to emphasize and illustrate the familiar tenet that neither charity nor forbearance must be carried to the point of permitting or condoning outrage.[10]

R. W. Chambers, in his British Academy lecture of 1937, had anticipated Miss Pope's carefully documented, carefully phrased analysis, by noting that Isabella was sternly Christian in her treatment of Claudio, and by comparing her behavior, favorably, to that of persons in Foxe's *Martyrs*.[11] Battenhouse, in his study of *Measure for Measure* (1946), had argued that the "holy Isabella," caught by the demands of Angelo prior to those of Claudio, was "like Christ in the wilderness."[12] And more recently, Madeleine Doran, in her book *Endeavors of Art* (1954), has partially joined forces with the theological-historical critics by asserting that our failure to look at Isabella from a Jacobean point of view toward chastity in women means that we

[10]In *Shakespeare Survey*, No. 2 (1949), pp. 77–78.

[11]"The Jacobean Shakespeare and *Measure for Measure*," *Proceedings of the British Academy*, XXIII (1937), 135–192.

[12]"*Measure for Measure* and Christian Doctrine of Atonement," p. 1046.

have "simply lost the key [to *Measure for Measure*], an easy thing to do in comedy."[13]

But it remained for the most ardent of the Christian apologists, Virgil Whitaker, to demonstrate logically (and inadvertently, it seems), that if you attempt to save *Measure for Measure* by regarding the Isabella who excoriates her brother as properly Jacobean-Christian, you are then caught out with the "other" Isabella who promotes the assignation between Angelo and Mariana. Whitaker presents in the strongest possible terms the notion that "much of the dismay with which modern readers view *Measure for Measure* is certainly due to its uncompromising adherence to fundamental Christian doctrines."[14] Isabella's "terrible dialogue with Claudio," he feels, "must be read against the full realization, perfectly obvious to any Elizabethan, that in demanding the life of his body at such a price Claudio is condemning his own soul to death as well as hers."[15] Whitaker admits the punitive sternness of the code, but insists that "it is undoubtedly Christianity."[16]

Whitaker, because of his insistence that Isabella "makes no...error in saying, in the presence of the law of God, 'Mercy to thee would prove itself a bawd; / 'Tis best that thou diest quickly,' " finds that "no argument can make acceptable the device by which Mariana substitutes for Isabella."[17] And we are back, by Whitaker's logic, where twentieth-century criticism started, with Quiller-Couch's feeling that the inadmissible element in *Measure for Meas-*

[13](Madison, 1954), p. 362.
[14]*Shakespeare's Use of Learning*, p. 218.
[15]Page 218.
[16]Page 218.
[17]Pages 219 and 221.

ure is Isabella's inconsistency as an exemplar of chastity. One can, of course, view the "other" Isabella as R. W. Chambers does, as "a sensible Elizabethan girl, with no nonsense about her,...[who] knows that it is no sin to bring husband and wife together."[18] Such a view is all very well if one wishes to substitute an avuncular cheerfulness for criticism; but it completely misses the point. If Isabella's treatment of her brother is to be robbed of its dramatic sting by being regarded as conventionally and punishingly Christian, then her treatment of Mariana, where mercy actually plays the bawd, should in all consistency be regarded as wholly diabolical.

Despite Miss Pope's scrupulous use of a limited historical evidence, and despite Virgil Whitaker's inner knowledge of what would have been perfectly obvious to any Jacobean, if one wishes to explore the Renaissance climate of opinion on sex as necessary to our interpretation of Act III of *Measure for Measure,* an equally good case could be made from Elizabethan-Jacobean religious writings for the easily forgivable nature of Isabella's yielding to Angelo. If one may be technical about it, a single act of intercourse between Isabella and Angelo would have been simple fornication, not adultery, to the early seventeenth-century theologians. And in both such a heavily intellectual study of the Seventh Commandment as that of Bishop Lancelot Andrewes in his posthumous *The Morall Law Expounded*[19] (1642), and in such popular studies as John Dod's *A Treatise or Exposition upon the ten commaundements, Grounded upon the scriptures cannonicall* (1603) and in John Downame's "A Treatise Against Fornication and Adulterie," (1609), simple fornication was considered the

---

[18]"The Jacobean Shakespeare and *Measure for Measure,*" p. 177.
[19](London), pp. 759–783.

least of the sexual sins. Moreover, since the moral effects
of fornication could be "quenched by true repentance"
(Dod)[20] or "prevented by hartie and unfained repentance,"[21] (Downame), it would surely have been perfectly
obvious to any Jacobean that the chances for Isabella's
soul, if she had yielded to Angelo, would have been good
indeed. She would most certainly have heartily repented
even in the very act of sex.

For what it is worth as evidence concerning some "average" point of view toward sex outside marriage which
might have been held by some "average" member of Shakespeare's audience, I note that there is much contemporary
evidence, voiced in semiofficial and in popular moral
tracts, which protested that average views were far too
casual. In the "Sermon against whoredom and unclean-
ness," from the Church of England Homilies (1595), sexual
vice is said to have "growen into such an height, that in a
manner among many, it is counted no sinne at all, but
rather a pastime, a dalliance, and but a touch of youth:
not rebuked, but winked at: not punished, but laughed
at."[22] Downame, in Chapter II of his "Treatise Against
Fornication," discusses "what fornication is, and of the
small account which worldings make of it."[23] In Arthur
Dent's *The Plaine Mans Path-Way to Heaven* (1603), the
character Antilegon, who voices the point of view of morally casual humanity, argues "Tush: whoredom is but a
tricke of youth: and wee see, all men have their imper-
fections."[24]

[20]Folio 54, verso.
[21]Page 144.
[22]Sig. K3^r.
[23]Page 132.
[24]Page 56.

If we consider either the intellectual or the aristocratic section of the early seventeenth century as a possible audience for *Measure for Measure,* it seems that our difficulties in imputing to this audience Isabella's notion that one's soul was the obvious forfeit for a single act of sex outside marriage are great indeed. In spite of the feelings of Battenhouse and Whitaker, surely Lucio's attitude toward the rebellion of a codpiece comes closer to views voiced by the young Donne, for example, the "great frequenter of Playes,"[25] than does Isabella's legalistic quibbling over my soul or your body. The sexual morality of the Elizabethan and Jacobean courtier—a Southampton, a Blount, a Raleigh—does not seem, on the record, to have been noted for its easy identification with so-called "normative" theological views. And there is no evidence of an Elizabeth Vernon, a Penelope Devereux, an Elizabeth Throgmorton being led fainting with remorse from a performance of *Measure for Measure,* after witnessing the bold defense by Isabella of her Christian chastity. If here and there an occasional "average" member of the original audiences for *Measure for Measure* (perhaps despite a private winking at sexual dalliance) would have felt publicly committed to Isabella's harsh views, it is difficult to believe that any appreciable number of the intellectual and aristocratic members of the audience would have felt so. The pleasure of being shocked at Claudio's request for life, and the pleasure of admiring Isabella's vitriolic denial of it, has been reserved for Christian nineteenth-century editors of *Measure for Measure,* and for a number of our twentieth-century historical-theological critics.

More important to an understanding of Act III.i than a

[25]Sir Richard Baker, *A Chronicle of the Kings of England* (London, 1643), p. 156.

scholars' debate over Isabella as the embodiment of an early seventeenth-century audience's special point of view toward sex, is the obvious fact that she exists solely as a character in a play. *Measure for Measure* is not a sociological document; it is a dubious tribute to Shakespeare to treat Isabella as an exhibit of average views. As Moody E. Prior has put it, in a classic statement of the critical problem involved:

The use of the Elizabethan audience as a critical norm seems almost by its very nature to create confusion. ... It tends to destroy the distinction between local success and greatness. But perhaps its most serious disservice is that it takes important critical questions out of circulation. ... It enters at precisely the point where serious and intelligent critical inquiry is most essential.[26]

Isabella, created to function in *Measure for Measure* as a novice on loan from a religious order, cannot be torn from the play to be held against theoretically re-established religious attitudes. The bases of her actions are dramatic, not theological. Her function is wholly within the play and there, most generally, as an interestingly difficult, complementary opposite to Angelo. The thing that sets Isabella off on her tirade against Claudio is not her orthodoxy. It is (as demonstrated in Chapters I and II) that she responds to Claudio's fear of death in a highly realistic, very human fashion when her own picture of herself is at stake. Isabella's steely Christian remarks about saving her soul from damnation are as appropriate to her character in the play as are those opposite ones of Mistress Ford in *The Merry Wives of Windsor* (II.i.49) who speaks jokingly of going "to hell for an eternal moment or so" for an affair with

[26]"The Elizabethan Audience and the Plays of Shakespeare," *Modern Philology*, XLIX (1951), 118.

Falstaff, or those of Emilia in *Othello* (IV.iii), who would venture adultery and purgatory for a sufficient price. Isabella requests Christian mercy for Claudio from Angelo. But to Claudio himself she becomes wholly judicial; she assumes, in her own defense, a Christian God concerned only with retaliation. It is her falling into Angelo's way of thinking, when she excoriates Claudio, that makes Isabella, momentarily at least, so like Angelo and carries the play to its climax, after which she will reverse herself.

Isabella's fear of immortal contamination by sex, in III.i, exists in a play which dramatizes, in a series of characters, a fairly complete spectrum of moral positions towards sex, and ones as recognizable to a Jacobean as to a member of a twentieth-century audience. The paradoxical element in *Measure for Measure,* as drama, is stepped up in intensity, certainly, by having a novice, almost vowed to perpetual chastity, one who wished for a greater restraint upon the members of her own chosen order, plead with her would-be seducer to excuse the natural sexual desires of her brother. Indeed, the brilliant and exciting conflict of attitudes between Isabella and Angelo is made possible by the fact that she is a novice. This fact also creates the even greater intellectual friction when she confronts Claudio. The audience's reaction to the crossing of attitudes between this second pair can best be described as a kind of emotional short circuit. And it is a short circuit which depends upon Isabella's conventual status. But if one insists upon an audience's identifying with her special way of looking, rather than with accepting the friction this scene generates, most of the carefully executed dramatic effect of her encounter with Angelo and then with Claudio is lost. If we wholly agree with Isabella's scorn of her brother in Act III, we may consider ourselves morally more orthodox than the eighteenth-century Mrs. Lennox and Samuel Johnson (or than Shakespeare's Duke Vincentio), who do not. But we have substituted either our own moral self-righteousness or our surrender to the historical annotator for the greater excitements of the play.

The neotheologians are far more interesting and subtle when they turn from a defense of Isabella as sternly "Christian" in her wishing her brother dead to assert that there are revealing and intended analogues between Biblical story and myth and the whole of *Measure for Measure*. Such assertions enable certain critics to accept the ameliorative Shakespearean version of the Renaissance story of the monstrous ransom and to explain the powerful impact of the play. Central to their analogical argument is the character of the Duke, who "like power divine" controls the individual destinies of all the other characters. Isabella's reference to Christ in her plea to Angelo for mercy to Claudio, the tone and mood of Juliet's penitence, Lucio's resemblance to Satan as tester, and a series of passages in the play in which fairly close Biblical parallels to plot and dialogue are claimed, make up the rest of the argument for "a religious basis" as inevitable "for the design of this particular play."[27] Sometimes the direct targets of the theological critics' ridicule are E. K. Chambers, Una M. Ellis-Fermor, and J. Dover Wilson, all of whom have detected a pessimistic or a cynical note in *Measure for Measure,* and have failed to sense the bright, serene, Christian atmosphere in the play.[28] Sometimes it is the more general critical notion of "something wrong" with *Measure for Measure* that acts as goad to their arguments. But the

[27]Nevill Coghill, "Comic Form in *Measure for Measure,*" in *Shakespeare Survey,* No. 8 (1955), 25.

[28]They are the targets for R. W. Chambers and for Nevill Coghill.

Christian apologists all agree that there is some kind of doctrinal-allegorical import to *Measure for Measure* even though they exhibit charitable disagreement toward each other as to the precise way in which this special import is to be defined.

G. Wilson Knight, as initiator of a Christian exegesis of the play in his *Wheel of Fire* (1930), compares the Duke to Christ, both as "prophet of a new order of ethics," and as one who "moves among men suffering grief at their sins and deriving joy from an unexpected flower of simple goodness." The play contains a "lesson driven home": that human justice is impossible because "man, himself a sinner [i.e., Angelo, but not the Duke?], cannot presume to judge." And Knight decrees that *Measure for Measure* "must be read, not as a picture of normal human affairs, but as a parable, like the parables of Jesus."[29] R. W. Chambers restates Knight's position by emphasizing the Christian, "more than human" mercy Isabella shows to Angelo (though not to Claudio). He concludes that in *Measure for Measure* we have been given "a noble [Christian] drama on the theme Judge not: for with what measure ye mete it shall be measured to you again."[30]

Roy W. Battenhouse, seeking "a proper [Christian] focus on *Measure for Measure*" in an area already explored by Knight and by Chambers, concluded that "the play can be made ultimately intelligible" by its "mysterious way of mirroring by analogy the cosmic drama of the Atonement."[31] Nevill Coghill, still pursuing Christian themes almost a decade later, argues that "the subject-matter [of

[29](London, ed. 1956), pp. 80, 82, 76 (see also Matt. vii, 1–6), 96.

[30]*Man's Unconquerable Mind* (London, 1938), p. 310.

[31]"*Measure for Measure* and Christian Doctrine of Atonement," pp. 1031, 1032, 1053–1054.

Measure for Measure] is sin," and that since "we live in a fallen world and yet have hope of salvation," *Measure for Measure* "is the comedy of Adam."[32]

More recently J. A. Bryant, Jr., in Chapter VI of his *Hippolyta's View: Some Christian Aspects of Shakespeare's Plays* (1961), has argued the "grave limitations" of regarding *Measure for Measure* as a mere play, a mere "tale of Vienna." In order to perceive its truly rich, poetic meaning one must view it as suggesting "the stage whereon man falls from grace, comes to know himself under the dispensation of Mosaic law, and finds redemption at last under a dispensation of grace with the return of his Lord in the full light of morning."[33]

At the level of their mere assertion as to what actually exists in *Measure for Measure* as evidence of its Christian design and meaning, one might well pick a series of small quarrels with each of the "findings" of the Christian apologists. The notion, for example, that an Anglican-Jacobean would (and that we should) see an obvious parallel between the Duke and Christ seems to me a fanciful exaggeration. The most obvious parallel to the Duke, to Shakespeare's audience and to one of the twentieth century, would surely be to the concept of an actual and worldly king, or other head of state, as God's very earthly representative. It would be not *to* power divine, as the neotheologians want it, but "like power divine," as *Measure for Measure* actually has it. It might also be, for many members of an early seventeenth-century audience, to King James himself (see Appendix). The tone of Juliet's penitence, beautifully and religiously awesome to Nevill Coghill because the play concerns sin, seems to me to be intentionally much more

[32]"Comic Form in *Measure for Measure*," pp. 25, 26.
[33]Pages 87, 107.

matter-of-fact, especially when one considers the Duke's later insistence that Angelo's and Mariana's coming together, in what must have been the coldest sexual encounter in Western literature, was no sin. And Coghill's and Bryant's further suggestion that Lucio, the friend of Claudio, the instigator of Isabella's plea for Claudio's life, is to be regarded as hidden out, in the thickets of the play's allegory, as Satan the tester, one would like to be able to toss to one of Lucio's admirers, Samuel Johnson,[34] for answer.

I would also have to reassert, against the findings of those who practice Christian exegesis on *Measure for Measure,* that Isabella's character is not meant mainly as symbol of Christian mercy throughout the play. She is surely meant to be interesting in herself as a dramatic character, not as representative of a theological view. She states a concept of mercy which perhaps reflects portions of Luke vi, and one certainly appropriate to her conventual longings. But Lucio's bawdy point of view toward sex is equally appropriate to his cheerful prurience. When Isabella is caught out in her personal predicament, she becomes wholly judicial (not symbol of mercy) toward her brother. And I would argue that *Measure for Measure,* though it uses them dramatically, can scarcely be said to "endorse" even her direct theological assertions concerning mercy in her discourse with Angelo. The mercy of Act V, moreover, is extended by the Duke to all participants in the moral decisions dramatized by the play, regardless of the degree of complicity of each in evil.

The denouement, moreover, does not involve us with a lesson of some kind but with an ameliorative view of

[34]*The Plays of William Shakespeare,* 8 vols. (London, 1765), I, 380, note 1. See also the general conclusion, p. 302.

human behavior—with, if you like, a *more* than Christian mercy. Indeed, it assumes that we will be susceptible to such a supra-Christian view, or this view could not function as the basis for the final stasis of the comedy. The mercy identified by Isabella with Christ in her encounter with Angelo, in the first half of the play, is identified with a new and secular understanding of Angelo, on her part, in the second half. Mercy is not taught us by Isabella, as Chambers and Coghill seem to think it is. Nor is it extracted from us by the total play. It is viewed first as Christian tenet, later as psychological insight. This second view is the ingredient necessary to make plausible (and therefore successful) the denouement to this most intellectual of Shakespeare's comedies.

Finally, if we follow Knight, Chambers, Coghill and company in feeling that we must read *Measure for Measure* as a parable with a lesson driven home, or as a play at least strongly buttressed with special Christian teachings, we are left with a serious aesthetic problem. Is a play which yields such a simple, definable meaning as that human justice is impossible, or that we should all go out of the theater exalted by a sudden vision of a more than human mercy, really a play at all? I would have to reiterate, against any such narrow "message" in the play, that *Measure for Measure* really attempts no solution of moral problems. As I see it (see Chapter II), the ironies and paradoxes of the play are not used to advocate a code of behavior, a "new order of ethics," as Knight insists.[35] They act in quite the opposite direction, to give us a sharper recognition of the complex nature of problems of moral decision. They give us a renewed sense that such problems are interesting

[35]*The Wheel of Fire* (ed. 1956), p. 80.

because they have permanent existence, not just in Shakespeare's Vienna, but also in the world outside.

The ultimate aesthetic question raised by the neotheologians, however, is larger and more significant than small quarrels as to whether we are intended by the play to agree with Isabella in wishing her brother dead, and whether we should prepare ourselves to regard the Duke as a Christ figure. The fundamental question is whether a rather dogmatically Christian or even a somewhat looser and mythically Christian analogue—e.g., the doctrine of the Atonement (Battenhouse), or the comedy of Adam (Coghill and Bryant)—can really be used to give a proper focus on *Measure for Measure,* or explain what is "wrong" with the play. Does either explain its power, our sense of the vast massive layer of implication under its intellectual and surface counterpoising of character and event?

The answer to this question is not ambiguous, despite the fact that the need to find a way to elucidate the powerful effects of *Measure for Measure* has driven a small school of modern critics to claim Christian analogues, whether or not they are there with the intention and force ascribed to them. My own very clear reaction is that the modern Christian apologist is strongly stirred by the play. But where a Coleridge understood it and recoiled from it for what it revealed concerning man's liability to sexual desire, the modern theological interpreter covers up the nature of the play's implications, shields himself from them. He prefers to take the meaning of the play out of the glaringly actual world of painful alternatives where Isabella, Claudio, and Angelo are revealed in their complete finitude, caught by anxious choice, into the cool shadows of institutionalized moral allegory or parable.

But then, what is Christian analogical thought supposed

to clear up in *Measure for Measure?* If analogy is applied to the play as a whole, or even to one or another character in a particular predicament, what more do we comprehend about this play? If we are told that its basic action is equivalent to, or almost to, or might have been thought by some "normative" Jacobean equivalent to the doctrine of the Atonement, is this a useful or a highly revelatory way of describing the basic plot element in *Measure for Measure,* the story of the monstrous ransom? Is it a useful way of verbalizing our sense of the undertow of implication and meaning which goes on under the intellectual surface of this comedy? Attempts to explain *Measure for Measure* by asserting equivalences between its action or its emotional power and dogmatic or mythical Christian doctrine or story fail because they do not add to its clarity or its implications. Such attempts are crude metaphors or similes of the whole, in which the play and the particular doctrine chosen by the critic are asserted as merely interchangeable, with neither one more fully illuminated.

In a more positive way, I would argue that all attempts to make *Measure for Measure* into an analogue of religious doctrine, or into some kind of religious allegory or parable, heavily restrict and contain its inferential power, and thereby diminish its ability to communicate. *Measure for Measure* is concerned with subtler values and perceptions about men and women than can be encompassed by gross religious assertions. If it has a deep relationship to religious thought, it rather suggests the clumsiness of an institutionalized concept of chastity or mercy or justice as a way of evaluating human conduct. Isabella's hot, womanish anger with Claudio, or the Duke's personal irritation with Lucio, or his ironic recognition that Angelo's evil has requited him well, do not suggest doctrinal Christianity so much as deeply felt, secular human feelings common to all, Christian or not.

Measure for Measure might be described as a play which takes conventional sexual morality seriously, but not because it is Pauline or part of a Judeo-Christian precept. It takes it seriously as part of the secular reality of the Western world in which we still live. One would also have to maintain, I think, that *Measure for Measure* treats the problem of human choice, where an Isabella, an Angelo, or a Claudio is caught out in the pitiless glare of everyday motivation, with far greater psychological insight than that in the official sixteenth- and seventeenth-century homilies of the Anglican church, or in Lancelot Andrewes' exhaustive analysis of the almost infinite possibilities for sexual sinning under the Seventh Commandment.[36] Whether *Measure for Measure* was written to appeal to a local audience's conscious or unconscious awareness of the doctrine of Atonement or the comedy of Adam and the Fortunate Fall seems, finally, a question of possible interest to the social historian viewing the play as document, but not to the literary critic. Even if such a local intention could be proved, it would still tell us too little of what we need to perceive in order to understand the power and force of the play.

In what terms, other than religious, should we explore the tentacular, deep-rooted strength of *Measure for Measure?* We part company with the Christian aestheticians reluctantly, because their words, if not winged, are always authoritative and therefore reassuring. Their view, as expressed most recently by Bryant, that in this play Shakespeare "recast a stodgily moralistic story in the context of

[36]*The Morall Law Expounded* (London, 1642), pp. 759–783.

an orthodox Christian vision,"[37] is certainly clear as an assertion, and one useful for examinations. But if there is a nexus between the import of *Measure for Measure* and the various Christian analogies and references claimed by one school of modern critics, it is not that the analogies reinforce some lesson of the play. It is that doctrinaire Christianity is used, by Isabella especially and occasionally by the Duke, as a mode of expression of insights concerning the ironies of human choice and human action which could be, or might be, expressed in other ways. The ironies have power over us (e.g., that Isabella is less merciful toward her brother than toward Angelo) not because they are expressed here and there in Christian phraseology or by Christian reference, but because they seem true.

If Virgil Whitaker were right, and Shakespeare had been as genuinely self-conscious a Jacobean-Christian in *Measure for Measure,* or in his other plays (as was George Herbert in his poems collected in *The Temple,* for example), we would be faced, we twentieth-century unbelievers, with a definable problem. We could only hope to make Shakespeare's plays come alive for us by transplanting old, lost religious belief into modern terms and views much as we translate the old terminology and belief in humors into modern psychological language and concept. Or we could turn to Empson for advice "as to how we can enjoy the literary expression of beliefs which we don't hold." Empson's solution could then be applied to *Measure for Measure* if the play were truly a densely orthodox religious vision. Empson's method would be for us, as audience, to imagine some other person holding the given lost beliefs, "an author or a character, and thus get a kind

[37]*Hippolyta's View* (Lexington, 1961), p. 107.

of experience of what their consequences (for a given sort of person) really are."[38]

Shakespeare's plays, however, as well as his poetry, are haunted by a restless, secular perceptiveness somewhat isolated from established religious orthodoxy. There is little in Shakespeare like the Christian optimism of Sir Thomas More or the religious pessimism of Fulke Greville. Indeed, if one compares the phrasing of the old *King Leir* printed in 1605 with Shakespeare's play, as Curtis B. Watson has done recently,[39] one is given the impression that Shakespeare must have been consciously intent upon neutralizing into a-religious language the conventionally religious reference and terminology found in the original. The plea against Time in the Sonnets is surely Ovidian, not Christian, in feeling as well as in occasional imagery. And *Measure for Measure* is in no way either a devotional or an allegorical writing, as these adjectives might be applied to Herbert's poem "The Collar," for example. It is a play which makes us intensely aware of the moments in time, in all their suggestiveness and complete secularity, in which mirror images of wholly human virtue and scorn are caught and explored in his dramatic characters. It is a play of men and women in a finite condition of anxiety, and then resolution, viewed well this side the "undiscover'd country from whose bourn/ No traveller returns."

One may concede to G. Wilson Knight, Whitaker, and Battenhouse that the moral sensibility in Shakespeare, and in his local audience, came into being and flourished in the rich, if decaying, soil of Renaissance Christianity.

[38]*The Structure of Complex Words* (London, 1951), p. 9.

[39]"Christian Themes in *King Lear* and in *King Leir,*" in *Shakespeare and the Renaissance Concept of Honor* (Princeton, 1960), pp. 362–366.

But one cannot concede the moral sensibility revealed in *Measure for Measure* to be in any way doctrinaire. Nor can one concede that Shakespeare's plays are generally intelligible to us only as we are able to see them as some theologically conventional mind of his day might possibly have seen them. Shakespeare's contemporary, the essayist and historian, the friend of John Donne, Sir Richard Baker (1568–1645), neatly and factually, I think, distinguishes the separate provinces of theology and drama as he saw them in the early seventeenth century, in his *Theatrum Redivivum,* published posthumously in London in 1662. His book was a reply to Prynne's *Histrio-Mastix* and could well serve as a seventeenth-century reply to our modern Christian apologists. Baker called plays "fit recreations for an honest Natural, or Moral man, but no ways to be matched with the high mysterious Contemplations of a Christian in Divinity." The purpose of writing a play was wholly secular, so that "as in a glasse, we might see the maners, and very Image of our daily life." Stage plays exist, he argues, "but to refresh our Spirits; but we hear Sermons to sanctifie our Spirits." A clergyman, Baker notes, "can never make a Glasse of a Pulpit, as we do of the Stage; that [i.e., a pulpit] may teach us to know ourselves, but cannot shew us to see our selves: this is only done by representation, which is the proper Office, and work of Plays."[40]

Attempts to impose Christian institutionalized moral codes and dogmas, or Christian analogues of story and myth, on Shakespeare's comedies and tragedies as if they were lost but essential elements for our understanding the plays, have little to recommend them except the personal intensity and sometimes the verbal grace of their perpetra-

[40]Quotations are from the 1670 edition titled *Theatrum Triumphans* and are on pp. 98, 130, and 133.

tors. The general ethical climate of *Measure for Measure* is undoubtedly Christian, with winds of Stoicism (as in the Duke's summation of the value of existence to Claudio in III.i) and of Aristotelianism (as in the Duke's insistence on virtue-in-action for both Angelo and Isabella) constantly blowing through it. But this is not to say the play exists to reinforce or to prove (or to be proved by) the limits set on mercy by spokesmen for Renaissance Christianity. It is not a parable which intentionally supports, or is supported by, theology. The vocabulary and the imagery of Western Christianity are, here and there, used as the language, the verbal vehicle of the play's existence. But the play's concern is with creating, in Baker's words, an epitome of the world's behavior, in which the means of discourse about mercy and chastity are, not unexpectedly, often theological.

A fundamental aspect of *Measure for Measure,* whether one happens to be pleased about it or not, is its appeal to human moral feelings older and deeper in Western civilization than the theorizing and dogmatizing about morality of doctrinaire medieval or Renaissance theologians. Even if all the "normative" members of Shakespeare's audience had left the Globe theater with rather literal thoughts about Othello's burning in hell or of Isabella's mercy being very Christ-like, this response (impossible to prove) would have been only their mode of verbalizing, creating an easy referent for, the turbulent feelings aroused in them by these very secular plays. In *Othello* they would have been responding to the desperate personal tragedy of one man's absolute and irredeemable loss of love *in this world.* In *Measure for Measure* they would have been responding to one woman's capacity to extract compassion and forgiveness from her insight into the effect of her own actions on those of her persecutor. ("I partly think / A due sincerity govern'd his deeds, / Till he did look on me.")

But neither play needs nor is given the support of official theological preoccupation with utter damnation or its counterpart, utter heavenly grace. Othello and Isabella are characters giving voice to the human condition, not to Christian theorizing and dogmatizing as to their immortal roles. And we are moved by the phrase from Othello, "O, I were damn'd beneath all depth in hell," and the use of the word "mercy" in *Measure for Measure* as they function in Shakespeare's dramatized secular world of actual murder and actual assignation. This key phrase and key word are the verbal symbols from the two plays of our sense of the possibility of both tragedy and redemption inside the knowable well-lighted, everyday world as it has been represented for us in *Othello* and in *Measure for Measure*.

Another way of putting it would be to say that Shakespeare's Isabella, like his Othello, his Hamlet, performs the actions and says the words in front of us by which she defines herself. There is created, in our presence, as we see or read *Measure for Measure*, a recognizable dramatic being, Isabella, about whom it may be convenient to a given critic to make discourse, to exchange interpretations, in Christian, in Freudian, in mythic terms and images. But she is essentially Isabella, and not Christ in the wilderness. Hamlet as he has recently been described by J. A. Bryant, Jr., is "the human, fallible, blind, tragic counterpart of the Christ who was knowingly both the scourge of evil and the sacrificial victim who willingly took that evil upon himself."[41] But this is only a wildly indirect way, compared,

[41]Page 121.

say, to the comment of Samuel Johnson, A. C. Bradley, or T. S. Eliot, of trying to fix in words some exchangeable sense of the vitality of Hamlet. The created central essence, the uniqueness of Hamlet or Isabella, is the all-important communicable object of our discourse. This uniqueness may suggest Christ to a critic immersed in theological speculation and the Oedipus complex to one immersed in psychological speculation. If we have sufficiently primitive minds, Hamlet and Isabella may stir uneasy feelings in us which lead us to want to discuss them in the role of scapegoat. But whatever they may be "like" to an individual critic, their fascination is that they are created as essentially themselves.

Shakespeare's plays, far from being directly or indirectly theological in outlook, dramatize character and event in quite another fashion. Without relating the phrasing to any formal philosophy, it can be said that character and event in Shakespeare appear before us as apprehended by the "timeless sensibility"[42] of an existential view of human life. Both Isabella, as she excoriates her brother and as she pleads for Angelo, and Hamlet as he reviles Ophelia with obscenities and as he fights with Laertes over her dead body, are dramatized before us to focus our own sensibility on the revelatory qualities of their actions and natures as individuals, not on the parable-like implications of these actions. It is the "beingness," the "revealedness" of Isabella and of Hamlet that is of dramatic importance. The prescriptive codes and regulations associated with Christianity are referred to, or often assumed, in both *Measure for Measure* and in *Hamlet*. They may serve to reinforce the dramatic intensity of these plays, but they

[42]Walter Kaufmann, *Existentialism from Dostoevsky to Sartre* (New York, 1956), p. 12.

are not themselves the central meaning. And neither play assumes or demands that one be a Jacobean-Christian to understand it.

The special, institutionalized Christian ordering of the unknowable, fathomless pool of time, on the surface of which we all float momentarily in the daily knowableness of our identity, is as obviously familiar to most members of Western civilization today as it was to the Jacobeans. But in *Measure for Measure* the verbal reminders of this Christian ordering of the unknowable—its moral values, rituals, doctrines, myths—are not ways in which Shakespeare asserts his personal orthodoxy (as Whitaker would have it); nor are they ways in which he appeals through the play to the orthodoxy of members of his audience. Mortimer R. Kadish has stated my own reaction to Christian exegetical aesthetics so clearly, in his essay "Sin, Science, and the Hard, Dry Style," that I quote a sizable passage from it:

Surely it is one thing to exhibit people in faith, prayer or enchantment—another to make the central action pivot about the metaphysical meaning of their state. This second alternative, to the displeasure of critics like Santayana, Shakespeare never takes. And, for that reason, recent attempts to provide for the Shakespearian drama a theological frame of reference miss the boat: as an artist, he has so structured his dramas that it does not matter to the play as such how he actually conceives or does not conceive his relation to divinity.[43]

Or, as Harbage has put it for Shakespeare's tragedies, "The adversary is not God but earthly sin, the origin of which is as open a question in Shakespeare as in the world about us."[44]

---

[43]*Philosophy and Phenomenological Research,* XIX (1958), 222.
[44]*As They Liked It* (New York, 1947), p. 151.

The characters in Shakespeare's plays may talk about themselves and explore their own private sense of being— a Richard II often, an Othello and an Isabella more occasionally—by referring to a Christian interpretation of things. But the Christian reference in Shakespeare is never presented, as it is by Spenser, for example, or in quite a different way by George Herbert, as a religious shield to mitigate a character's intense awareness of the harsh ordeal it is to come to terms with the nature of everyday being. In such a tragedy as *Hamlet,* the hero attains a knowledge of the quality of his life at the cost of his life. Isabella, in *Measure for Measure,* attains an intuitive consciousness of the very genuine potency of the "prone and speechless dialect" of her femininity, not tragically, but by a bitter ordeal. But neither *Hamlet* nor *Measure for Measure* is intimately involved with, or dependent upon, Christian knowledge or Christian belief. The denouement, the moment of final stasis in these plays, is not complicated with metaphysical intimations or consolations, Christian or otherwise. What is held brightly in focus is an excited and intensified sense of the immediate knowableness of a created and complex being: a Hamlet, an Isabella.

Chapter V

The Achievement of Shakespeare's *Measure for Measure*

IT is surely a curious notion, though currently still a fashionable one, that the full act of literary criticism of *Measure for Measure* is largely an act of historical retrieval, whether the retrieval be that of the special and limiting literary tastes of Shakespeare's time or of the special ways in which his age differs from ours in regarding chastity or providence. Most members of Shakespeare's audience—or of Chekhov's or of Shaw's—were no doubt caught up in local religious opinions and other commonplaces of their day, entangled by them in their thought and talk, and in their way of regarding the life they found themselves in the process of living. But Shakespeare's plays have obviously survived their local origins, as Samuel Johnson noted long ago,[1] and largely because they do not dramatize merely the local and the transient views: in T. S. Eliot's words, those "impersonal ideas" of an age "which obscure what we really are and feel, what we really want, and what really excites our interest."[2]

Wellek and Warren have remarked of Shakespeare, in their *Theory of Literature,* that as critics "we are not primarily interested in what he has in common with...all men of the Renaissance, all Elizabethans.... We want rather to discover what is peculiarly Shakespeare's...and this is obviously a problem of individuality and value."[3] Yet too much of our contemporary criticism has actually led us away from all that *is* peculiarly Shakespeare's in *Measure for Measure.* When we face the complex dramatic design of the play and the subtleties of implication to be derived from a close, scene by scene scrutiny of it, we find that analyses of its local Elizabethan legal and moral proprieties give us a meager critical discourse indeed. Such discourse assumes that Shakespeare, in *Measure for Measure,* is (as T. S. Eliot put it adversely for Tennyson) "almost wholly encrusted with parasitic opinion, almost wholly merged into his environment."[4] But such an assumption fails utterly, I think, as explanation of the unique individuality and value of *Measure for Measure* from which emerges its powerful impact on us as a play.

[1] *The Plays* (London, 1765), Preface, I, Sig. A2ʳ & ᵛ.
[2] "Blake," in *The Sacred Wood* (London, 1960 ed.), p. 154.
[3] (New York, 1949), p. 6.
[4] "Blake," p. 154.

If we cannot make do with a criticism which would "explain" *Measure for Measure* as an object merely in need of historical reconstruction and restoration, as a possible alternative we may simply affirm without interpretation and analysis the feeling that there is much in the play that is richly inferential and profound. This too is a rather sorely limited kind of response. It is a kind aptly described by Wayne Shumaker as "confined to parts of the consciousness able to express themselves only by ambiguous ejaculations."[5] The only adequate alternative, then, is to present a truly full-scale analysis of all that seems relevant and discussable within the play. My own interpretations and views of *Measure for Measure* have been an attempt at such a full-scale analysis. They do establish, I think, a sufficiently substantial referent for the play's greatness. And any effort to reach an adequate definition or verification of the play's achievement requires that one always keep this full-scale referent consciously in mind.

It is appropriate, therefore, to summarize in brief my own full view of this play as a preliminary to a final evaluative statement concerning the achieved content of *Measure for Measure*. It is, first of all, idiosyncratic in many ways, and it has a special identity apart from Shakespeare's other comedies. As I have indicated in Chapter I, it is Shakespeare's most ingeniously constructed comedy. In *Measure for Measure,* but in no other of his comedies, the plot design is as schematically balanced as are the moral paradoxes.

Another of the identifying peculiarities of *Measure for Measure,* explored earlier in Chapter II, can be suggested by saying that the relationship between the emotional states

[5]*Elements of Critical Theory* (Berkeley and Los Angeles, 1952), p. 71.

of the principal characters and the intellectual concepts they express or stand for is the obverse of that found, for example, in *Twelfth Night*. In the latter play, the emotional turmoil of Duke Orsino, Viola, and Olivia is kept constantly before us. The romantic attitudes and concepts underlying this amorous turmoil are implied, but they are almost never stated. In *Measure for Measure,* on the other hand, it is the attitudes and concepts themselves (concerning the degrees of legality and mercy to be applied to sexual indulgence) which are kept before us. It is this intellectualizing surface of the play which immediately catches our attention. Our apprehension of the ambiguous relationship between what the characters say and admit, their devotion to ideas and concepts, and what they actually do, comes as a residual, unstated implication. If the peculiarity of the character Viola is that she is presented from the beginning of the play as emotionally *in medias res,* the peculiarity of Isabella (as well as of Angelo and the Duke), is that she is presented, from the beginning, as intellectually *in medias res.* The emotional intensity of *Measure for Measure* comes less from our direct confrontation by characters in an emotional state than from the crosscurrents of feelings and tensions in its characters which we understand by inference.

Further, *Measure for Measure* is unique as Shakespearean comedy in that it puts a deliberate emphasis on early seventeenth-century Jamesian views (analyzed in the appendix following this chapter). The Duke, the play's largest single role, is created as a ruler who has read and remembered much of what James I had to say, especially in his book of 1603, *Basilicon Doron:* concerning the place of a king in the political and religious spheres, his powers to act outside statutory law, the nice distinctions to be observed in applying his twin powers of mercy and justice. One might also guess that the transformation of Isabella from a novice of the Order of St. Clare to the presumptive wife of the Duke was also part of the new, Jamesian interest in Protestant Christianity which had produced the Hampton Court Conference of 1603, and was to produce the King James translation of the Bible. It represents the "natural" middle way of Anglican views. "Luther the monk, like the Duke, took a wife."[6] Isabella is returned to the secular world.

But beyond these specific components of the play is the insistently frank treatment accorded sex throughout *Measure for Measure*. This treatment is also one of its peculiar and distinguishing features. Its tone is heard most noticeably in the language of Lucio and in the boldness and coldness of the dialogue between Isabella and the Duke as they arrange the assignation between Angelo and Mariana in Act III, and as they discuss it in Act V. It comes close to that found in the plays written by Shakespeare's contemporaries for what Harbage calls "the rival tradition" of the Elizabethan-Jacobean coterie theater, the tastes of which "were sufficiently jaded or exploratory (according to the point of view) to require the fillip of the excessive, the devious, the perverse." This is not to say that in *Measure for Measure* we see an attempt on Shakespeare's part to crowd his lines (as Marston had done in *The Fawne* and in *Sophonisba,* or as Middleton had done in *The Phoenix* or in his *Family of Love*) with a "succession of sexual novelties," and with a "wide range of perverse

[6] Denton J. Snider, "Shakespeare's *Measure for Measure,*" *Journal of Speculative Philosophy,* IX (1875), 425.

suggestion."[7] It is merely to observe that *Measure for Measure,* unlike Shakespeare's romantic comedies or his love-game comedies, involves us directly and almost continually in imagery associated with, and in comment on, the act of sex. This involvement, obviously, is wholly deliberate, wholly intentional.[8]

Another special fact to hold in view when considering *Measure for Measure* is that the plot constantly leads us into expectations which it does not fulfill. As Shakespeare's recasting of the Renaissance story of the monstrous ransom, it leads us, at first, to expect a dramatic skit resolving one of those arbitrary questions posed so often in Medieval and in Renaissance literature: whether it were better for a woman to sacrifice her virginity or her brother's life. But part of the identifying individuality of the play is that the question is never answered. The climactic scene between Isabella and her brother, in which she voices her choice, is carefully ambivalent as to the intended direction for our moral sympathy. And both Isabella's chastity and Claudio's life remain intact at the play's end, despite her choice. What emerges in *Measure for Measure* from its failure to resolve the posed question is a series of reversals in point of view by its main characters: in Claudio, after the climactic scene with Isabella, the sudden appearance of an overpowering sense of guilt and shame, and a wish to die swiftly; in Isabella, an unexpected resolution to save her brother's life by playing bawd to Angelo and Mariana; in

[7] *Shakespeare and the Rival Traditions* (New York, 1952), pp. 208 and 210.

[8] Eric Partridge comments, in *Shakespeare's Bawdy* (London, 1947), p. 54: "*Measure for Measure* and *Othello* are Shakespeare's most sexual, most bawdy plays.... Quantitatively there is very little to choose between them."

Angelo, a final acknowledgment of his own liability to error. What is kept brightly alive for the audience to the play's end, by the play's side-stepping the posed question, is an intense awareness of moral dissonance.

In conjunction with its other individualizing traits, the ameliorative, lenient ending to *Measure for Measure* has a strangeness about it which also acts to separate this play from Shakespeare's other comedies (unless we consider his *Troilus and Cressida* to be one). It is not, as Swinburne once maintained,[9] that there is a confusion of aim here, as between comedy and tragedy. Northrop Frye has put as an elemental difference between the two forms of drama the fact that "the sense of reality is. . . far higher in tragedy than in comedy, as in comedy the logic of events normally gives way to the audience's desire for a happy ending."[10] And it seems obvious, despite Swinburne and some of the play's eighteenth-century critics, that the sense of reality in *Measure for Measure*, with its Duke in the role of final arbiter, "like power divine," is never allowed to become strong enough for tragedy.

The lingering strangeness of the "happy" ending to the play has been prepared for with careful artistry and at comedy's usual expense of a logic of events. It resolves happenings which "in reality" might seem too violent for comedy if the play did not ask us, finally, to view them as purely theoretical ones. The play, at least on its intellectual surface, remains one of ideas, where much has seemed to have occurred, but where nothing much has actually occurred. No individual's interest in life has been terribly diminished by the events of the play, as in *Lear* or in

[9]Algernon Charles Swinburne, *A Study of Shakespeare* (London, 1880), pp. 202–205.

[10]*Anatomy of Criticism* (Princeton, 1957), p. 75.

Othello.[11] The characters of *Measure for Measure,* at its close, are presented as men and women on the verge of change, anticipating positive actions. The ending is not on a joyous, festive moment, as in Shakespeare's earlier comedies. But it is a satisfying ending to the events of the play, if a unique one in Shakespearean comedy, because it resolves the discordant clash of events by suggesting a generic and forgivable culpability in all men.

These cumulative, interrelated idiosyncracies out of which *Measure for Measure* has been constructed may make it seem the most difficult of Shakespeare's plays to define as comedy. But these very idiosyncracies create its insistent demands on a moral awareness in us far deeper than that provoked by his other comedies. Where *Twelfth Night* persuades us to surrender to a golden world of romance by its formalized gaiety, and where *The Tempest* persuades us to accept its easy accommodation to evil by the richness of its nostalgia for innocent youth and by its autumnal tone, *Measure for Measure* achieves its comic power over us by dramatizing its events with the seriousness of tragedy, but without the harsh, unyielding "reality" of tragedy. Perhaps we could best identify *Measure for Measure* as a comedy wholly in an ironic mode: it suggests no serious, realizable solution to the moral dilemmas it has dramatized, but it comes to an end by implicating all of us in the perception that moral dilemma is a part of the human situation.

I choose, then, to call Shakespeare's *Measure for Measure* his greatest comedy (though obviously not his greatest play). This evaluation is based on all of the play's richly

[11]Cf. Lily B. Campbell, "Bradley Revisited," *Studies in Philology,* XLIV (1947), 180: "Death itself is not so terrible as the loss of the will to live which we see in each of the great tragic heroes of Shakespeare."

intricate components analyzed here, which merge to invite our fascinated response. Unlike Shakespeare's love comedies which lightly evoke romance, or lightly tease it, this play, to borrow a phrase from Lionel Trilling, is deeply concerned with "the recalcitrant stuff of life."[12] Moreover, the art of the play is sufficiently hard at work with this "recalcitrant stuff" to reveal it to us with the intensity and power whereby we are compelled to call the play great.

This "stuff," the basic substance of *Measure for Measure,* the area of human reality blocked out for dramatization in the play, is the tantalizing excitement, the fear, the shame of man's sexuality, his shared common denominator of sexual desire. The two central actions continually discussed in the dialogue of the play are the consummation of sex between Claudio and Juliet and between Angelo and Mariana. The great moral-legal rhetoric between Angelo and Isabella, in which mercy and justice are given a full-blown utterance, is also wholly focused on the act of sex. Claudio's memorable phrases describing Isabella's power to move men, Angelo's description of the "strong and swelling evil" of his desire, Lucio's flippant evaluation of lust as the "rebellion of a codpiece," even the Duke's self-analytical "he was not much inclin'd that way," are phrases directly sexual in reference. The play is a dramatization of a little world of conflicting voices and attitudes toward sex, a world in which the characters discussing the "thirsty evil" are shown as fully articulate in their reactions. They exist as characters involved in the recalcitrant sexuality shared by all men and who have problems with it because they inhabit the secular world where it thrives.

The art of the play whereby this obstinate sexual sub-

[12]"The Meaning of a Literary Idea," in *The Liberal Imagination* (New York, 1950), p. 297.

stance is made important to us, attains its power over us, comes basically from the startlingly and insistently ironic ways in which the play presents event and character. The surface events of *Measure for Measure* occur in a proper chronological sequence. But they are always in the process of leading to other events which are opposite to those apparently intended. The characters in *Measure for Measure,* moreover, are not only involved in events which reach unintended conclusions. Their behavior in the face of these events is a violation, a teasing mockery of our sense of expectation as to how these characters ought to, or will, respond.

The ironies of event, in *Measure for Measure,* explored in the first chapter of this study, need no further elucidation here. But the play's artfully successful exploitation of our sense of the expected, in the reactions of its characters, needs a final comment. At the surface of our minds we expect "correct" and stereotyped responses from them. We expect, in company with Isabella and the Duke, that Angelo will release Claudio once he has found importunate sex in himself and has indulged it with Mariana. But he does not. We expect that Isabella who pleads mercy to Angelo will treat her brother (after the fashion of Whetstone's Cassandra) with a tender solicitude which will prevent his asking for his life. But she fails us. We assume that Lucio will continue his role of witty friend to Claudio and advisor to Isabella to the end of the play. But he survives in the second half as one who delights in almost unmotivated slander. We assume that the Duke, who "contended especially to know himself," will remain dispassionate to the end. But he reveals himself capable of a final, highly personal, intemperate outburst against Lucio.

In *Measure for Measure,* the reactions of these characters

violate our unthinking sense of expectation, but persuade us simultaneously of the appropriateness of the violation. The play receives a major excitement and intensity *because* Angelo's superficially unexpected fear of retaliation from a living Claudio, and Isabella's superficially unexpected hatred for her brother, actually satisfy in us an unvoiced, unthought, insinuated apprehension concerning the nature of these two. Lucio's alterations in behavior startle (and therefore delight) our expectations even as they violate them; and we adjust to his outrageous slander of the Duke easily enough. The Duke's sensitive, angry response to Lucio's sexual accusations against him, if it frustrates what we might have expected, at the same time excites our final interest in the Duke. He is revealed, suddenly, as capable of human reactions less exalted, less detached than any he has hitherto displayed.

Central to the art of *Measure for Measure* is the fact that it is a deliberately "uncomfortable" play, one which carefully exploits our own easy, surface response to its substance by forcing us to adjust to a level of apprehension of motives for human actions which lie far deeper than we are usually willing to go. Its way of looking at human sexuality is to show it as always subject to an accustomed discipline by statutory law and orthodox morality. It also shows it as operating within individuals from depths of instinctual feeling only superficially contained by the boundaries of orthodoxy. Isabella's, Angelo's, Claudio's, Lucio's decisions and reactions are dramatized as existing within a world which assumes a certain moral certitude. But the play does not flatter our "correct" views in sexual matters by keeping us within safe range of such certitude. It does not move us by the obvious. The power of the play comes from its terrifying invitation to us to go beyond certitude. It invites us to recognize both the elemental, instinctual nature of sexual desire and at the same time to recognize that it both mocks, and is mocked by, the private disguises of love and morality which individuals impose on themselves, and which are imposed upon them by society.

The heavily ironic mode of *Measure for Measure* acts as the major artistic device in the achievement of its content, its sexual "stuff," because out of the friction developed by its paradoxical way of looking comes a sense of a tremendously enlarged moral perspective. Robert Tener, in a study of irony as a tradition of comedy, has described with consummate skill this process by which irony forces such a new perspective to come into existence in an individual. The "emotional dissonance" created within the spectator by the "vis comica" of irony and paradox, he argues, brings about an emotional state in which "he is bothered and even pained at times by what he feels. At this immediate threshold of emotional pain the spectator has only begun to have a vague interaction with paradoxes. Continued stimulation causes him to broaden his perspective as he sinks into a cushion of his experiences and associations. These in turn enlarge the depth and scope of his interaction [with the play] as he begins to transform the conflicts to yet higher levels of meaning and finds a multiplicity of identifications possible."[13]

Coleridge, in his violent reaction to *Measure for Measure,* one might guess, stopped at the first stage of emotional dissonance as described by Robert Tener, and was unwilling to go beyond what bothered and what

[13]"The Phoenix Riddle: A Study of Irony in Comedy" (unpublished dissertation, Western Reserve University, 1965), p. 68. Tener's comment is an extension of the views of Alan Reynolds Thompson, in *The Dry Mock* (Berkeley, 1948), pp. 11, 15, 19.

pained him (almost his own words) in it. Walter Pater, on the other hand, was able to transform the conflicts of the play to what Tener calls a higher level of meaning, and to attempt to verbalize this meaning:

It is for this finer justice, a justice based on a more delicate appreciation of the true conditions of men and things, a true respect of persons in our estimate of actions, that the people in *Measure for Measure* cry out as they pass before us. . . . In its ethics it is an epitome of. . .the moral judgments of an observer. . .who. . .knows how the threads in the design before him hold together under the surface.[14]

As audience, then, we have been jostled and goaded by ironies of event and by ironies of expectation throughout *Measure for Measure*. It is this assault on our conventional moral certitude, on our superficial and conventional views of ourselves and of others, in matters of sex, that provokes in us a feeling that we have a surer knowledge of the actuating forces from which moral choices truly emerge.

Measure for Measure, finally, is a comedy which unlocks our most profound awareness of the nature of an ineluctable evil in man. It is not evil as defined by prohibitions of church and state, not a post-lapsarian and expected evil. It is the evil in man contingent upon his human predicament. It is evil viewed as a destructive element in everyone, the latent capacity of Isabella, of Angelo, even, finally, of the Duke (to Johnson's dismay), to unleash angry, retaliatory "justice" in order to maintain his personal place or role in society, his own ego intact. The play achieves its great penetrating power, its great moral intensity, because it allows us to win for ourselves this knowledge even of ourselves.

[14]"Appreciations," in *The Works of Walter Pater* (London, 1901), V, 183–184.

Appendix

The Historical Dimension in *Measure for Measure:* The Role of James I in the Play[1]

MEASURE FOR MEASURE made an explicit appeal to its own age by the fact that its Duke is very Jamesian, very much concerned, from beginning to end, with what he calls the "properties" of government and with "sufficiency" in office. Early seventeenth-century political attitudes and assumptions, indeed, are part of the fabric of this comedy,

[1] With a few minor differences in wording, this Appendix originally appeared as an essay in *ELH*, XXVI (1959), 188–208.

and a very deliberate part, because they are wholly Shakespeare's addition to his principal source for the play, Whetstone's *Promos and Cassandra.* We tend to view the Duke in his omnipotence as wholly a given device in the comedy, a part of the play's arbitrary dramatic design. He has the longest single role, and his omniscience, we feel, is essential to the play's schematic structure. But *Measure for Measure,* by means of its Duke, does contain a radical dimension of local Jacobean reference, a radical historical dimension, essential to take into account in any attempt at a full apprehension of the play.

One of the curiosities of our twentieth-century criticism is that the Tudor political theory embedded in Shakespeare's history plays has been so completely demonstrated (by Lily B. Campbell and by Tillyard) that we have almost forgotten those other elements in these plays that make them still viable for us. With *Measure for Measure,* however, we have been so concerned with its "meaning" that its demonstrable use of Jamesian political views has gone largely unremarked. Elizabeth M. Pope's discussion of the play in her article, "The Renaissance Background of *Measure for Measure*,"[2] is an important exception, however. She has made it abundantly clear that *Measure for Measure has* a political aspect, and that it reflects conventional Renaissance attitudes toward matters of state lost to a contemporary audience unschooled in Jacobean history. Shakespeare's presentation of the conflict between mercy and justice in the play, and his dramatization, in Duke Vincentio, of the powers and obligations of a prince, she shows to be related to discussions of such matters in Renaissance theological treatises and in Jacobean sermons.

[2] *Shakespeare Survey,* No. 2 (1949), pp. 66–82.

She has suggested, further, that the inclusion of such material in *Measure for Measure* was in conformity with a popular taste in political ideas. It was a part of the "outburst of concern with the theory of government [which] seems to have been inspired primarily by the accession of James."[3]

Miss Pope's thesis that Shakespeare, in *Measure for Measure*, is properly Jacobean in his treatment of political theory seems beyond dispute. But if we turn to the play itself, and examine in sharper focus its use of political ideas and attitudes, we find that *Measure for Measure* is much more than a casual and fortuitous reflection of Renaissance political views. It is a play in which the political element bears the conscious and unmistakable imprint of the predilections of James I himself as Shakespeare and his London audience were aware of them in the first flush of the post-Elizabethan era.

Even though it is today somewhat extrinsic to our interest in *Measure for Measure*, it is not difficult to see why Shakespeare might have been prompted to add a Jamesian political element to his source story. Theatrical enterprise, then as now, was highly competitive, and the greatest asset of his acting company in 1603–1604 was its new status as the King's men. As one of the principal directing members of this company, Shakespeare undoubtedly wished to foster its recently acquired royal sponsorship and to encourage, if possible, a direct personal attachment of the King for the royal players. Shakespeare may even have felt under some obligation to identify his first Jacobean comedy with the ideas of the new ruler. At any rate, he seems to have deliberately sketched in Duke Vincentio a character whose

[3]"The Renaissance Background of *Measure for Measure*." p. 70.

behavior as a ruler would be attractive to James because it followed patterns the King had publicly advocated. In addition, Shakespeare made a fairly general appeal throughout the play to his audience's obvious interest in the concepts of the new Stuart political order. He did this by incorporating into the action of *Measure for Measure* a series of James's known attitudes toward government, including the King's great personal fascination with the conflicting demands of mercy and justice in achieving order in the state.

The evidence which demonstrates the role of James I in *Measure for Measure* takes its validity from two assumptions not difficult to make. The first is that the text of the play as we have it, surviving only in the Folio edition, is essentially that of the production at court before King James, in 1604.[4] The second assumption is that from the spring of 1603, with the death of Elizabeth, to the production of *Measure for Measure* at court about a year and a half later, James I during "this most balmy time" was the most talked about person in London, the "observ'd of all observers." His character, his personality, his political utterances were so much in the public gaze and mind in part, no doubt, because he was the first new monarch England had had in a generation, and in part because he had almost miraculously succeeded to the throne without bloodshed, and "incertainties" had crowned "themselves assured." But beyond these obvious things, James had certainly been vain enough to want his ideas on statecraft to be discussed, both because he was King and because he thought of himself as an intellectual. And he had deliber-

---

[4]See "Revels Account," in E. K. Chambers, *William Shakespeare* (Oxford, 1930), II, 331. See also J. W. Lever, "The Date of *Measure for Measure*," *SQ*, X (1959), 381–388.

ately advertised himself to his new English subjects as a poet and a scholar, as well as a statesman, by releasing for London publication, in 1603, all his major literary, religious, and political writings.[5]

The most obvious evidence that Shakespeare incorporated a current interest in James in *Measure for Measure* has been in the public domain since the eighteenth century. But its authenticity has remained clouded by the doubts of reputable scholars. It is the "fact," first remarked by Thomas Tyrwhitt in 1766,[6] that two passages in this play (and a related third which has gone unnoticed) reflect in a flattering way a publicly known distaste on James's part for displaying himself before shouting, unruly London crowds.

The first of the passages is from the Duke's initial self-characterization, addressed to Angelo and to the audience as he takes abrupt leave from his newly appointed deputy:

> I'll privily away. I love the people,
> But do not like to stage me to their eyes.
> Though it do well, I do not relish well
> Their loud applause and Aves vehement;
> Nor do I think the man of safe discretion
> That does affect it. [I.i.68]

The second of the passages is part of Angelo's comparison of his feelings of suffocation with desire for Isabella with a

[5](1) *His Majesties Lepanto, or, Heroicall Song;* (2) *A Meditation Upon...the First Booke of Chronicles;* (3) *A Fruitefull Meditation, Containing a Plaine...Exposition...of the Revelation;* (4) *The True Lawe of Free Monarchies, or, The Reciprock and Mutuall Dutie Betwixt a Free King, and his Naturall Subjects;* (5) *Basilicon Doron, or His Majesties Instructions to his Dearest Sonne;* (6) *Daemonologie, in Forme of a Dialogue.*

[6]*Observations and Conjectures Upon Some Passages of Shakespeare* (Oxford, 1766), pp. 36–37.

king's feelings of suffocation when pressed upon by a foolish
swarm of gapers:

> So play the foolish throngs with one that swounds;
> Come all to help him, and so stop the air
> By which he should revive; and even so
> The general, subject to a well-wish'd king,
> Quit their own part, and in obsequious fondness
> Crowd to his presence, where their untaught love
> Must needs appear offence. [II.iv.24]

The third passage, hitherto unnoticed by editors, shows the
Duke, on his return to Vienna, remembering his own
initial adverse comment to Angelo on the "Aves vehement"
of his people. He therefore seeks to excuse his new willingness to display himself to his subjects. In his soliloquy, the
Duke states that he will explain this about-face to Angelo
by the fact that:

> ...I am near at home
> And that, by great injunctions, I am bound
> To enter publicly. [IV.iii.99]

Both H. C. Hart[7] and E. K. Chambers[8] have doubted
the somewhat scanty evidence cited by Tyrwhitt and the
eighteenth century that James had a dislike for crowds.
And some contemporary editors[9] of *Measure for Measure*
still annotate the pertinent passages from the play so warily,
and with such cautious equivocation, that one cannot tell

[7]*Measure for Measure,* The Arden Shakespeare (London, 1905),
p. x.

[8]*William Shakespeare,* I, 453.

[9]E.g., Neilson and Hill, *The Complete Plays and Poems,* p. 390;
Hardin Craig, *The Complete Works* (1951), p. 833; Davis Harding,
Measure for Measure, The Yale Shakespeare (New Haven, 1954),
p. 125.

whether they think the evidence insufficient as to James's reactions or as to Shakespeare's intentions. Fortunately, however, one seventeenth-century report of James's behavior, which Tyrwhitt missed and which has been wholly overlooked by Shakespeare's editors,[10] actually shows the King, very early in his reign, explicitly, vocally, and very publicly annoyed by what he considered the "untaught love" of his new English subjects. It is Gilbert Dugdale's *The Time Triumphant* (1604).[11]

This pamphlet contains an extended and dramatic account of James's spontaneous outburst against what he considered the unruly English mob's failure to keep its distance from his person and a proper decorum in his presence, in a sudden appearance which he made in the London streets, prior to his coronation. And I quote from it at some length to convince all waverers. Dugdale first notes that James was curious to see at first hand the street decorations being erected to honor his royal procession to Westminster to be crowned. He took coach to the Exchange, therefore, "desirous privately. . . to visit them," and "thinkeing to passe unknowne." But:

the wylie Multitude perceiving something, began with such hurly burly, to run up and downe with such unreverent rash-

[10]But not by Sir Charles Firth. See *Stuart Tracts, 1603–1693, An English Garner* (Westminster, 1903), pp. xi–xii.

[11]*The Time Triumphant, Declaring in briefe, the arival of . . . King James, . . . His Coronation* (London, 1604). The quotations occur sig. B2ʳ to sig. B3ᵛ. I have partially repunctuated and recapitalized Dugdale's wretched text. Dugdale, a kinsman of Robert Armin of the King's men, is the first to note in print the honor accorded Shakespeare's company by James's "taking to him the late Lord chamberlaines servants now the Kings acters" (sig. Bᵛ). Lever (see note 4 above) thinks that Armin may have collaborated in writing *The Time Triumphant*.

nes, as the people of the Exchange were glad to shut the staire dores to keepe them out. Heare they lost the pleasing sight they might have enjoyde but for their rashnes.

The King commended the behavior of the merchants of the Exchange who, "like so many pictures...stood silent;" but "discommended the rudenes of the Multitude, who regardles of time, place, or person will be so troublesome."

Dugdale, sensing that the new Jacobean world was to be a less boisterous one than that which had cheered Elizabeth,[12] and perhaps also hoping to flatter James into noticing him, adds a solemn admonition:

countrymen, let me tell you this: if you hard what I heare as concerning that [i.e., the King's reaction], you would stake your feete to the Earth at such a time, ere you would runne so regardles up and downe. Say it is [his] highnes pleasure to be private, as you may note by the order of his comming, will you then be publique and proclaime that which love and duty cryes silence too? This shewes his love to you, but your open ignorance to him. You will say perchance it is your love. Will you in love prease uppon your Soveraigne thereby to offend him, your Soveraigne perchance mistake your love, and punnish it as an offence? But heare me. When hereafter [he] comes by you, doe as they doe in Scotland: stand still, see all, and use silence. So shall you cherish his visitation and see him, thrice for once amongst you. But I feare my counsell is but water turnd into the Tems. It helps not.

Finally, Dugdale lets go his comments on James with a flight of fancy as to the King's thoughts during the actual

[12]Contrast Shakespeare's cheerful sketch of the "Aves" of the Elizabethan Londoners welcoming an Essex, *Henry V*; V, Prologue, 11. 22–34, Cf. Arthur Wilson, *The History of Great Britain, Being the Life and Reign of King James the First* (London, 1653), pp. 12–13; "He was not like his Predecessor...that with a well-pleased affection met her peoples Acclamations."

coronation procession making its tortuous way through the crowded streets of London. Dugdale halts his narrative to let us see James once more at the Exchange, and remarks that, "his highness being right over the Exchange, smilde looking toward it, belike remembering his last being there, the grace of the Marchants, and the rudenes of the multitude."

Tyrwhitt's evidence that James had an aversion to displaying himself in public was based upon Sir Simon D'Ewes's comments, in 1621, and David Hume's eighteenth-century conjectures.[13] It has remained more tantalizing than conclusive to editors of *Measure for Measure*. If, however, we add to Tyrwhitt's speculation Dugdale's graphic account of James's two visits to the Exchange, it seems fair to assert as a historical fact[14] that the King had a very real and well-known dislike of the "unreverent rashnes" and the "rudenes" of the "wylie Multitude" of London. If we were still to assume, after reading Dugdale, that the three references in *Measure for Measure* to a ruler's antipathy to the "Aves vehement" of the crowd were fortuitous elements of dialogue and characterization on Shakespeare's part, we would at least have to grant that the King, Dugdale if he saw the play, and a good many

[13]Tyrwhitt's evidence was: (1) a passage from Sir Simon D'Ewes' autobiography of 1637 describing James's behavior toward crowds in 1621 (Harleian *ms.* No. 646, British Museum, fol. 54ᵛ); and (2) an edict of James forbidding access of crowds at one point on his journey from Edinburgh to London. The edict is discussed in the anon. *The True Narration of the Entertainment of his Royall Majestie* (London, 1603), sig. D2ʳ; Tyrwhitt's interpretation is based on David Hume, *History of Great Britain* (Edinburgh, 1754), I, 2–3.

[14]D. Harris Willson, in his *King James VI and I* (London, 1956), p. 165, speaks of James's aversion to crowds as fact, but curiously cites no evidence.

members of the audience would have thought otherwise.

One might observe that Shakespeare makes use of James's adverse reaction to crowds in two rather different ways, in *Measure for Measure*. The remarks of the Duke are made to seem in character, whereas those of Angelo are not. Angelo's comparison of his feelings of compulsive lust (II.iv.24) for Isabella to a fainting man's being smothered by excited onlookers is strained. His extension of the comparison to the effect a swarming horde has on a king is sheer metaphorical decoration, and carries the intent of the comparison beyond the obvious dramatic needs at that moment of the play.[15] Angelo, indeed, seems to step out of his role of would-be seducer in order to rationalize (momentarily, to be sure) the point of view of James himself (Angelo says "a King," and there are no kings in Vienna), rather than to enlarge our conception of what he, as a character in the play, is actually feeling. His speech, therefore, may be considered as direct eulogy of James's feelings. As such, it is a brilliant tour de force in empathy, a flawless rendering, in a few lines, of the sense of claustrophobia, of the fear of being trapped,[16] that a person of James's temperament might be assumed to have experienced on public display, when surrounded and pressed upon by his admirers in "obsequious fondness."

The Duke's reflections of James's attitude of repulsion

[15]It might be argued that Angelo's sympathy with the feelings of kings makes him less of an outsider, and his redemption more agreeable.

[16]The trapping of James and the murderous attack on him by Alexander, the brother of the Earl of Gowrie, may have helped make James timid and suspicious of people for the rest of his life. See *The Earle of Gowries Conspiracie against the Kings Majestie* (London, 1603).

toward a surging crowd, however, are of a subtler nature. They are made to seem dramatically appropriate to this ruler of Vienna who has "ever lov'd the life removed," and act as an interpretation or rationalization of James's personal feelings, suggesting both to the audience and to the King that these feelings come from the highest ethical motives. A ruler who responds to such street demonstrations as the Duke describes is not a man, in the Duke's words, "of safe discretion." He is permitting himself to be "affected" out of mere vanity, and may swerve from a right and considered course of action. The initial remarks of the Duke concerning a ruler on public display, then, lack the gratuitous element of Angelo's lines: they carry the normal weight of dialogue intended to create in us a sense of the Duke's character in the play. And, one observes, Shakespeare continues throughout the play to create the Duke in the mold of James's ideal prince. He feeds into the Duke's lines sententious utterances on morality and on the proper role of an absolute prince to make him a character with whom the new King of England, and his interested admirers in the audience, would find it hard not to agree.

Less directly obvious evidence that Shakespeare created a Duke of Vienna whose views would seem appropriate ones to James lies in Shakespeare's demonstrable use of the King's book on statecraft, the *Basilicon Doron,* or "Kingly Gift," as a source for the Duke's ideas.[17] This book, ad-

---

[17]Louis Albrecht, in his *Neue Untersuchungen zu Shakespeares Mass für Mass* (Berlin, 1914), presents a long discussion (pp. 129–216) of the interrelationship of *Measure for Measure, The Basilicon Doron,* and James I. He points out that George Chalmers, in 1779, and later scholars, had preceded him in suggesting *The Basilicon Doron* as a source for Duke Vincentio. Albrecht then compares parallel passages from King James's *Basilicon Doron* and *Measure for*

dressed by James to his son, was published in London for the first time in March of 1603, within a few days of Elizabeth's death. It was, as nearly as James could make it, a detailed statement of his own concepts of the correct role of a divine-right king in matters of religion, the state, and in things "indifferent." Further, James had taken care to admonish his readers that his *Basilicon Doron* "must be taken of al men, for the true image of my very minde, and form of the rule which I have prescribed to my selfe and mine."[18] The public's interest in it (and no doubt Shakespeare's) is indicated by the fact that it had no less than four separate editions in 1603 alone.[19] With James's permission

---

Measure, some of which I have compared, as has also Elizabeth M. Pope (see note 2 above). W. W. Lawrence finds himself "not convinced by Albrecht's parallels" (*Shakespeare's Problem Comedies,* p. 108 and p. 245, note 35). My own feeling is that Albrecht is right in assuming Shakespeare's awareness of *The Basilicon Doron* when he was writing *Measure for Measure,* but that his analysis of his materials is not careful enough to be convincing by itself. He uses parallel citations, Tyrwhitt's comments, etc., to prove *Measure for Measure* an act of homage ("Huldigungsakte") on Shakespeare's part to the new King James at his coronation (pp. 164 and 204). He finds *Measure for Measure* to have been utilized by Shakespeare as a kind of mirror for magistrates ("als einen Fürstenspiegel," pp. 193 and 204). Shakespeare's Duke is an artful character-portrait, a personification of James (pp. 175 and 199). Shakespeare, in addition, idealized Ann of Denmark in Isabella (pp. 205–210). He later portrayed James in Prospero (pp. 241–244). The supposed "amicable Letter" to Shakespeare from King James (see E. K. Chambers, *William Shakespeare,* II, 270) was probably a note of thanks for Shakespeare's homage to James in creating the play *Measure for Measure* (p. 298).

[18]Sig. B3^{v}.

[19]See *The Basilicon Doron of King James VI,* ed. James Craigie, Scottish Text Society, 2 vols. (Edinburgh and London, 1944 and 1950), II, 142–149.

it was turned into curious, aphoristic verse in this year (under the title, *A Princes Looking Glasse*) by one of its academic admirers, William Willymat of Cambridge.[20] Its popularity is further suggested by the references to it in the writings of such diverse Jacobean spokesmen as Samuel Daniel, Richard Martin (who had received the dedication of Davies' *Orchestra*), and William Camden.[21] Francis Bacon's dispassionate summary (c.1610) that it was a book which "falling into every man's hand filled the whole realm as with a good perfume,"[22] is sufficiently typical.

It would have been difficult for Shakespeare in 1603–1604, both as a literate individual and as leading playwright for the new King's men, to have ignored James's self-portrait in his *Basilicon Doron*. And Norman Nathan, for example, in an article "The Marriage of Duke Vincentio and Isabella,"[23] simply assumes Shakespeare's use of the book in *Measure for Measure* as fact, in order to argue (perhaps a bit thinly) that the Duke's proposal of marriage

[20]*A Princes Looking Glasse...excerpted and chosen out of... Basilicon Doron* (Cambridge, 1603). Willymat confesses "I againe and againe read it over" (sig. A3^r).

[21]Daniel, in *A Panegyrike Congratulatorie to the Kings Majestie* (1603), st. 20, refers to "those judiciall lines" of the *Basilicon Doron*. Martin, in *A Speach Delivered, To the Kings...Majestie in the Name of the Sheriffes of London* (1603), sig. B2^r, speaks of the King's "sound bookes now fresh in every mans hands, beeing (to use your Majesties owne wordes) the *Vive ideas* or representations of the mind" (this last a quotation from *Basilicon Doron*, sig. A8^r–A8^v). Camden, in *The History of...Princess Elizabeth* (London, ed. 1675), p. 564, remarks, "Incredible it is how many mens Hearts and Affections he wone unto him by his writing of it and what an Expectation of himself he raised amongst all men, even to Admiration."

[22]*Literary and Professional Works* (Vol. I in *The Works,* ed. Spedding, Ellis, Heath [London, 1878], VI), pp. 278–279.

[23]*SQ*, VII (1956), 43–45.

to Isabella at the end of the play is no mere rounding out of the action with paired couples. The Duke's choice of a wife he sees as a conscious reflection of James's expressed ideas in the *Basilicon Doron*[24] as to the kind of woman a prince should marry and as to the propriety for a ruler of an unromantic approach toward matrimony.

Nathan's thesis is based upon rather sketchy statements in *Measure for Measure,* and if the Duke's attitude toward marriage were the only echoing of the King's ideas in the play, at most we would concede that the James of the *Basilicon Doron* would not have disapproved the Duke's choice. But the accumulation of such echoes in *Measure for Measure,* reflecting other, less amorphous points of view of James, especially as they are used to characterize the Duke, finally defeats skepticism, and forces us to realize that Shakespeare carefully mined the *Basilicon Doron* to dramatize the intellectual interests of his new patron. We are further convinced that Shakespeare grafted the role of the Duke on to his source, in part at least, to create a character in whom to embody these interests.

An early example in *Measure for Measure* of Shakespeare's attributing to the Duke ideas on matters of state which James had expressed in his *Basilicon Doron* occurs at I.i.30, where in a loose, but I think deliberate, paraphrase of James's assertions, the Duke admonishes Angelo that virtue in a ruler must be in an active state. Nature, the Duke argues, lends superior qualities to men only as she expects some tangible return, or "use," from her investment. As to Angelo,

> Thyself and thy belongings
> Are not thine own so proper as to waste

[24]See *Basilicon Doron,* pp. 72–82.

> Thyself upon thy virtues, they on thee.
> Heaven doth with us as we with torches do,
> Not light them for themselves; for if our virtues
> Did not go forth of us, 'twere all alike
> As if we had them not.

The Duke's observations, not startling in themselves, could scarcely have been more appropriate in a play of 1604, produced at the court of the King who had specified, in his advice to his son, that

It is not enough that ye have and retaine (as prisoners) within your selfe never so many good qualities and vertues, except ye employ them, and set them on worke, for the weale of them that are committed to your charge: *Virtutis enim laus omnis in actione consistit*.[25]

The Duke's harsh reaction to Lucio's slanders, I think, is another example of Shakespeare's incorporation into *Measure for Measure* of James's own expressed and insistent convictions. The Duke, disguised as a Friar, first gives voice to outrage against Lucio's idle, scandal-mongering remark that the absent ruler "would mouth with a beggar, though she smelt brown bread and garlic":

> No might nor greatness in mortality
> Can censure scape; back-wounding calumny
> The whitest virtue strikes. What king so strong
> Can tie the gall up in the slanderous tongue?
> [III.ii.196]

[25]*Basilicon Doron,* p. 61. James, in a side note, appropriately refers his comments to Aristotle, and the Latin phrase to Cicero. See also James's comment in *Flores Regii: Proverbs and Aphorismes...Spoken by his Most Excellent Majestie,* collected by F. L. S. (London, 1627), p. 127: "It is not sufficient...onely to eate, and drinke, and make an even reckoning at the yeares end...for wee are not in the world for fruition, but for Action."

And, in the last scene of the play, the Duke justifies his punishment of Lucio's behavior with the terse comment: "Slandering a prince deserves it" (V.i.530).

James had expressed a closely similar and harsh irritation in the *Basilicon Doron* at the petty slanders a king must endure from his irresponsible subjects. His estimate of the honesty and reliability of the "wylie Multitude" in passing judgment on the actions of a ruler is very like his estimate of the significance of their public applause. He thus writes, with personal impatience, "unto one fault, is all the common people of this Kingdome subject...which is, to judge and speake rashlie of their Prince." As an expedient against the slanders of "unreverent speakers" James advocated the course of the law. Ideally, however, he thought the proper remedy against "unjust railers" (like Lucio) was "so to rule, as may justly stop their mouthes from all such idle and unreverent speeches."[26]

It is certainly part of the integral comic design of *Measure for Measure* that Lucio should fall so neatly into the hands of the Duke he had slandered. And Lucio's role as comic realist in the play is sufficiently evident. Shakespeare's use of so outrageously unreverent a railer as Lucio as a foil for the Duke is surely also as much a calculated attempt to please James (and an audience aware of James's attitudes) as are the play's references to the "Aves vehement" of the crowd. One may conclude that Shakespeare,

[26]*Basilicon Doron,* pp. 52–53. Willymat picked out James's castigation of slanderers to versify in *A Princes Looking Glasse,* Bk. II, sts. 32–33. In *A Loyal Subjects Looking Glasse* (London, 1604), Willymat reiterates James's attitude, speaking of "incorrigible felowes, these beliers, and virulent exclamers on such as are in authority," and who seek "to deprave their sufficiency." He concludes that "they are worthy of death" (pp. 31–33).

in allowing Lucio first to aggravate the Duke in the extreme and then to be caught, was anticipating, at least in part, what he hoped would be the King's personal delight in Lucio's exposure.

Another of the characterizing attributes of the Duke in *Measure for Measure* seems imitated from the *Basilicon Doron,* and is somewhat more positive than an irritation with personal slander. It is the Duke's conviction that a king should, in his own person, be a model of the kind of virtue he expects from his people. Escalus partially expresses it in his thumbnail sketch of the Duke, at III.ii.246, describing him as "one that, above all other strifes, contended especially to know himself." James had used this phrase in his excited greeting of Sir John Davies, in 1603, as "Nosce Teipsum."[27] The Duke himself, as part of his soliloquy at the end of Act III, states this conviction explicitly:

> He who the sword of heaven will bear
> Should be as holy as severe;
> Pattern in himself to know,
> Grace to stand, and virtue go;
> More nor less to others paying
> Than by self-offenses weighing.

To be sure, the Duke's remarks are directed against the hypocrite Angelo, and are an obvious bit of moralizing in context. But they are also an echo of the sense of many passages in the *Basilicon Doron.* The following two concerning virtue in high place are fairly typical of James's

[27]According to Anthony à Wood, Davies accompanied Lord Hunsdon to Scotland to greet James. On hearing Davies' name, "the king straitway asked, whether he was *Nosce Teipsum?* and being answered that he was the same, he graciously embraced him" (*Athenae Oxoniensis,* ed. Philip Bliss [London, 1815], II, 400–406).

statements. The first has to do with what the Duke had called "pattern in himself to know":

And as your company should bee a paterne to the rest of the people, so should your person bee a lampe and a mirrour to your companie: giving light to your servants to walke in the path of vertue, and representing unto them such worthie qualities, as they should preasse to imitate.

The second of the passages from the *Basilicon Doron* is from the opening sentence of Book I, and concerns judging others by one's own behavior, what the Duke had phrased as "self-offenses weighing":

he cannot be thought worthie to rule and commaund others, that cannot rule and dantone [i.e., subdue] his owne proper affections and unreasonable appetites.[28]

The Duke's picture of himself as something of a recluse, a man partially withdrawn from the world and given to scholarship, is a further example of Shakespeare's consistent mirroring of the *Basilicon Doron*. This aspect of the Duke's character reflects an uncommon and self-conscious intellectualism in a ruler that would make him, one can only suppose, additionally appealing to James. Thus, at I.iii.7, the Duke describes himself to the Friar as a meditative prince:

> My Holy sir, none better knows than you
> How I have ever lov'd the life removed
> And held in idle price to haunt assemblies
> Where youth, and cost, witless bravery keeps.

Again, in defending himself from Lucio's "unreverent speeches," and specifically from Lucio's charge that the absent Duke was "a very superficial, ignorant, unweighing fellow" (III.ii.147), the Duke, speaking of himself in the third person, says in nettled protest: "Let him be but

[28]Pages 83–84.

testimonied in his own bringings-forth, and he shall appear to the envious a scholar, a statesman, and a soldier" (III.ii.152).

The Duke, as a scholarly, studious ruler, was no doubt very like the person Shakespeare and his contemporaries had ideally pictured the new King to be. This was true, in part, because the *Basilicon Doron,* with its running side-notes, had an air of the academy about it. In addition, James's analysis of the nature of government, in *The True Law of Free Monarchies,* would have been ample demonstration to Shakespeare and his audience that at least the King thought of himself as a scholar and statesman. Indeed, James's pride in his own "bringings-forth" was obvious, and paid constant tribute by literate Englishmen other than Shakespeare in the opening years of the new century. William Barlow, for example, in his published report of the Hampton Court Conference (1603), had referred to the King as "a Living Library, and a walking Study."[29] Richard Martin, Master of the Middle Temple, in his "Speach...to the King" (1603), had called James a living example of Plato's philosopher-king.[30] Bilson, in his "Coronation Sermon," was careful to note that he spoke before a "learned King."[31] And Sir Richard Baker, who had been knighted by James in 1603, described him in his *Chronicle* as "next being a King, he was made to be a Scholler."[32]

[29]William Barlow, Bishop of Lincoln, *The Summe and Substance of the Conference...in his Majesties Privy-Chamber, at Hampton Court,* January 14, 1603 [i.e., 1604] (London, 1604), p. 84.

[30]Sig. B2ᵛ.

[31]Thomas Bilson, Bishop of Winchester, *A Sermon preached at Westminster before the King and Queenes Majesties, at their Coronations* (London, 1603), sig. C3ʳ–sig. C3ᵛ.

[32]*A Chronicle of the Kings of England* (London, 1643), p. 143. See also James's statement, *Flores Regii,* item 175, p. 151: "He that is

It seems apparent, therefore, that the Duke's claims to a scholarly nature were no chance bits of dialogue in Shakespeare's first Jacobean comedy, but were rather related to a current of flattery, lapping about James, and a further effort by Shakespeare to create in this Duke a character with whom it would be pleasant for James to agree.

Of course, neither the Duke of Vienna nor James Stuart was startlingly original in the choice of attitudes and ideas they have in common.[33] Nor could one assert any connection between these two on this basis were it not that the date of *Measure for Measure* coincides so nicely with that of the *Basilicon Doron*, and with James's entry into England. But this conjunction in time, it seems to me, makes it impossible to believe that Shakespeare, just by odd luck, had created a Duke of Vienna who agreed with the new King not only in his dislike of the "Aves" of the crowd, but also in his concept of virtue-in-action, his irritation at the "unreverent speeches" of the common people, his insistence that a ruler should first subdue his own appetites before he attempted to subdue them in his subjects, and his wish to appear to the "envious," in his "own bringings-forth," both a scholar and a statesman. And I will end this series of parallels by noting, without further comment, the hint of Shakespeare's title for his first new comedy before the King (and Duke Vincentio's repetition of it, V.i.416) on the third from the last page of the *Basilicon Doron*, where James advises his son: "And above all, let the measure of your love to every one, be according to the measure of his vertue" (p. 152).

---

not a Philosopher, governs by guesse, and will prove a dangerous statesman."

[33]Craigie, ed., *Basilicon Doron*, II, 63–87, discusses the sources of James's ideas.

Further evidence of the role of James I in *Measure for Measure* is more general and less specifically related to the character of the Duke. It comes from the fact that, in so far as this play concerns itself with problems in governing, it deals with ones which had an obvious interest to the new King, and therefore to Shakespeare's audience in general. Thus the thematic question in *Measure for Measure,* as to the proper relationship between mercy and justice, was one in which James had displayed considerable public interest in the years 1603 and 1604. This interest is demonstrable both in James's theoretical analysis of this relationship in the *Basilicon Doron* and in his demonstration of his theories in action in his journey from Edinburgh to London to take the throne.

In Book II of the *Basilicon Doron,* "Of a Kings Dutie in his Office," James had argued a temperate point of view toward the letter of the law from which Angelo's behavior, in attempting to enforce immoderate justice against Claudio, would have seemed both tyrannous and revolting. James had summarized: "use Justice, but with such moderation, as it turne not in Tyrannie: otherwaies *summum ius,* is *summa iniuria*" (p. 85). Further, Angelo was not using the kind of judgment that should accompany absolute power. In picking out the statute against fornication to enforce literally, he ran counter to James's basic premise that statutory laws "are ordained as rules of vertuous and sociall living, and not to be snares to trap your good subjects: and therefore the law must be interpreted...not to the literall sense thereof. *Nam ratio est anima legis* (p. 86). One is therefore tempted to think that if Shakespeare had created a Duke to seem particularly appealing to James, Angelo as deputy, in James's phrase tyrannically "counterfeiting the

Sainte" (p. 25)[34] in his use of statutory law as a snare to trap a good subject, was created to seem particularly evil. (Escalus observes [II.i], "this gentleman/ Whom I would save had a most noble father.")

In his journey to London in 1603, indeed, James had put theory into action. As the new King, he had publicly dramatized a personal interpretation of the ageless conflict between mercy and justice, choosing an incident which had occurred on the way as a kind of case in point. As carefully reported in the anonymous *The True Narration,* a cut-purse was taken "doing the deed" at the King's temporary court at "New-warke upon Trent," April 21, 1603. The King saw his chance to demonstrate his theories, and, abruptly:

his Majestie...directed a Warrant, presently...to have him hanged.... The King ere he went from New-warke, as hee had commanded this Silken base theefe, in justice to bee put to death, so in his beninge and gracious mercie, he gives life to all the other poore and wretched prisoners, clearing the Castle of them al.[35]

The widespread public interest in this assertion first of justice, and then of mercy, was indicated not only by its inclusion in the pamphlet *The True Narration,* but also by its impact on Sir John Harington, for example. Harington, recording his reactions in his "Breefe Notes and Remembraunces," makes a more than usually acid comment on

---

[34]Cf. James's further statement, p. 29: "And as for the execution of good lawes, whereat I left, remember that among the differences that I put betwixt the formes of government of a good King, and an unsurping Tyrant; I shew how a Tyrant would enter like a Saint while hee found himselfe fast under-foote, and then would suffer his unrulie affections to burst foorth."

[35]*True Narration,* sig. E1v–E2r.

James's little demonstration.[36] And Sir Richard Baker, looking back on James's reign, recorded the King's action at New-warke as one of some moment, noting the irony that this "unseasonable delinquent...would force the K.[ing] to commit Justice at a time when hee intended nothing but mercy."[37] I think the incident but one more of the many curious parallels in time between James's expressed ideas and publicly known behavior,[38] and the thematic ideas used by Shakespeare in *Measure for Measure*.

Another of the problems of governing taken up in *Measure for Measure*, though less directly central to the structure of the play than that of mortality and mercy, is concerned with the plight of a ruler (Duke Vincentio) who has allowed the "strict statutes" of the law to go unenforced for "fourteen years."[39] After such a lapse, the Duke explains to Friar Thomas, the statutes are

[36]*Nugae Antiquae*, selected by Henry Harington, 2 vols. (London, 1804), I, 180: "I heare our new Kynge hathe hangede one man before he was tryede; 'tis strangely done: now if the wynde blowethe thus, why may not a man be tryed before he hathe offended?"

[37]*Chronicle*, p. 122. See also John Stow, *The Annales of England* (London, 1605), p. 1431.

[38]Chapman's estimate of James's interest in justice and mercy is implicit in his letter written to the King in 1605, pleading forgiveness for *Eastward Hoe*. Chapman appeals to James's "most Cesar-like Bountie (who Conquerd still to spare the Conquerd: and was glad of offences that he might forgive)" (*Letter Book*, Folger Library *ms.* No. 420423, fol. 88ʳ; see also *Athenaeum*, March 30, 1901, p. 403).

[39]B. Frank Carpenter, in his introduction to the Bankside-Restoration edition of *Measure for Measure* (New York, 1908), calls attention to Francis Bacon's concern with penal laws "that have been sleepers of long" in his essay, "Of Judicature." Bacon's phrasing and concept is occasionally close to Shakespeare's. Cf. Isabella's plea, *Measure for Measure*, II.ii.34–41, with Bacon's "In causes of life and death judges

> ...more mock'd than fear'd; so our decrees,
> Dead to infliction, to themselves are dead,
> And liberty plucks justice by the nose. [I.iii.27]

The Duke remarks, further, that

> Sith 'twas my fault to give the people scope,
> 'Twould be my tyranny to strike and gall them. [I.iii.35]

This specific problem raised by the Duke as to when a ruler should be strict and when lenient was also intended to interest James, I think, as he had discussed this difficulty and had suggested a solution to it, in the *Basilicon Doron*. James confesses that he himself had thought, at the start of his rule in Scotland, "(by being gracious at the beginning) to winne all mens hearts to a loving and willing obedience." He complains that his theory went awry, however, and that his excessive mercy achieved "the disorder of the countrie, and the losse of my thankes to be all my reward." He therefore advises his son that when he becomes king, he begin by punishing without clemency all infractions of the law. This is to let his people know that "yee can strike, then may yee thereafter all the dayes of your life mixe justice with mercie." But if (like the scholarly Duke of Vienna) he should exercise "clemencie at the first," the offenses

would soone come to such heapes, and the contempt of you growe so great, that when yee would fall to punish, the number of them to be punished would exceed the innocent... and against your nature would bee compelled then to wracke manie whome chastisement of few in the beginning might have preserved.[40]

---

ought (as far as the law permitteth) in justice to remember mercy, and to cast a severe eye upon the example, but a merciful eye upon the person."

[40]Pages 30–31. Willymat elects to versify these ideas (*A Princes Looking Glasse,* Bk. II, st. 8).

A further result of Shakespeare's observance of the various ways in which James reacted to statutory law may help explain a lapse in the dramatic structure of *Measure for Measure*. The Duke, having turned power over to Angelo so that old laws might be enforced once more, thereafter seems to lose all interest in these laws, and they are not referred to at all in the long denouement of Act V. I think it more than coincidence that just as the Duke lets go the stated problem of law enforcement which motivates his departure from Vienna, and becomes completely fascinated by the behavior of Angelo, his deputy, so James in *his* writings on government, though he discusses the need to enforce statutory law, seems to be as casually indifferent as Duke Vincentio to the results of such enforcement. He advises his son: "remit everie thing to the ordinarie judicature for eschewing of confusion: but let it bee your owne craft, to take a sharpe account of every man in his office."[41]

The similarity between the Duke's and James's somewhat cosmic attitude toward statutory law is based upon the fact that both had declared themselves above, and somewhat apart from it. The Duke makes his position clear in turning power over to Angelo:

> Your scope is as mine own,
> So to enforce or qualify the laws
> As to your soul seems good. [I.i.65]

This is a fairly terse rendering of James's own widely publicized position in regard to the powers of a divine-right king. In *The True Law of Free Monarchies*, for example, James's summary of these powers is a detailed statement of Duke

---

[41]*Basilicon Doron*, p. 92. See also *Flores Regii*, item 23, p. 20: "The wisdome of a King is chiefly seene in the election of his Officers, as in places which require a peculiar sufficiencie."

Vincentio's generalities. James argues that a ruler ought to be tolerant of the law, but that he is under a personal obligation to qualify it as circumstances vary:

The King is above the Law, as both the author, and giver of strength thereto. . . . And where he sees the law doubt-some or rigorous, he may interpret or mittigate the same: least otherwise *Summa ius* be *Summum iniuria.* . . . And therefore general lawes, made publikely in Parliament, may, upon knowne respectes to the King, by his authoritie be mittigated, and suspended upon causes onely knowne to him.[42]

A final piece of evidence that James I's predilections were mirrored by Shakespeare in *Measure for Measure* lies in the fact that the Duke is never more like James's concept of a king than in his bland assumption of his personal right to interfere in the lives of all subordinate persons. The Duke's arranging for Mariana's assignation, his concealment of the fact that Claudio is alive, his willingness to play a monk even to the point of hearing confessions of people about to die, was all very Jamesian. The role of the king, as pictured in the *Basilicon Doron,* was that of a "naturall father and kindly maister" (p. 25) of his subjects. In *The True Law of Free Monarchies,* James had stated that a king was literally "a Judge set by God over them [the people]," having "power over the life, and death of every one of them" (sigs. C5^r and D^r). And everywhere in his writings James assumes his right, as King, to take on himself not only secular power but also any religious power he wishes, remarking in one passage to his son that

[42]*True Lawe of Free Monarchies,* sig. D^v. Cf. Bilson's flattering repetition of this concept; "What private men may not touch without Theft and Murder, that Princes may lawfully dispose, as Gods Ministers" ("Coronation Sermon," sig. B4^v).

"ruling them [i.e., the clergy] well, is no small point of your office."[43]

It is a Stuart divine-right Duke who looks on Angelo's evil deeds "like power divine,"[44] and who plays the Stuart role of an earthly God in the fifth act, keeping the truth from everyone until it suits his personal whim that it should be known. This autocratic quality in the Duke, indeed, has led Robert G. Shedd to point out (appropriately) that the Duke's behavior resembles that of James himself when he decided to play with the lives of the men connected with the Ralegh conspiracy (1603).[45] For a contemporary's account of James's God-like teasing of these men, I quote from Baker's *Chronicle:*

...this was the course which the K. [ing] held in showing mercy. After the death of the three before named he signed three other warrants for the execution of the late L. Cobham,

[43]*Basilicon Doron,* p. 89. Cf. James's reply to Knewstubs, as reported by Barlow, *The Summe and Substance,* p. 70: "I will have one doctrine and one discipline, one Religion, in substance, and in ceremony: and therefore I charge you, never speake more to that point, (how farre you are bound to obey?)." Cf. Bilson, "Coronation Sermon," sig. B5^r–B5^v: "They [princes] are Fathers by Gods Law, that have or should have fatherly care over us, whether it be to ayde us in the things of this life, as masters and teachers; or to guide us the true way to heaven, as pastors and ministers...." King James's supremacy over the Church is asserted in *Constitutions and Canons* (London, 1604), Sects. I and II.

[44]Barlow reports James as identifying himself with Christ at the Hampton Court Conference: "I may say of my selfe, as Christ did of himself: Though I lived among them...I was never of them" (*The Summe and Substance,* p. 74). James is quoted as saying "Clemencie is a Divine instinct, and worketh Supernaturall effects" (*Flores Regii,* item 199, p. 170).

[45]"The *Measure for Measure* of Shakespeare's 1604 Audience" (University of Michigan dissertation, microfilm, 1953), pp. 172 ff.

the Lord Grey, and Sir Griffin Markeham, on a certain day then following; but before that day came he privately framed another warrant, written with his own hand to the Sheriffe; (who was then Sir Benjamin Tichburne,) by which he countermanded the former Warrants: and that there might be no notice taken of it: he sent it by Mr. John Gybbe...one utterly unknown to all the company, appointing him to deliver it so, that it might not take effect, till after their severall confessions, and at the very point of their Execution, which was accordingly performed: At which time, it was a wonderful thing to see how the Delinquents falling on their knees, lamented their misdoings, and most of all how they extolled the Kings unspeakable mercy.[46]

Sir Richard Baker's account reminds one not only of the Duke's James-like detachment as he looked upon

[46]Pages 125–126. Cf. Sir Dudley Carlton's description, quoted in Lucy Aikin, *Memoirs of the Court of King James the First*, 2 vols. (London, 1822), I, p. 174: "So as Grey and Markham, being brought back to the scaffold, as they then were...looked strange one upon the other, like men beheaded and met again in the other world. Now all the actors being together on the stage (as use is at the end of a play), the sheriff made a short speech unto them, by way of interrogatory of the heinousness of their offences, the justness of their trials, their lawful condemnation and due execution there to be performed, to all which they assented; then saith the sheriff, 'See the mercy of your prince, who, of himself, hath sent hither a countermand and given you your lives.' There was no need to beg a *plaudite* of the audience, for it was given with such hues and cries, that it went from the castle into the town."

James's actual letter of clemency is quoted in William Sanderson, *History of Mary, Queen of Scotland, And of Her Son and Successor James* (London, 1656), pp. 287–288. See also John Stow's account, *Summary of Chronicles* (London, 1604), pp. 452–453; that of John Speed, *The History of Great Britaine* (London, 1614), pp. 885–886. For a denunciation of Raleigh et al., see Richard Johnson, *Lanterne-light for Loyall Subjects* (London, 1603), sigs. B3^v–B4^r.

Angelo's passes, but his equal detachment in keeping Isabella "ignorant of her good/ To make her heavenly comforts of despair/ When it is least expected" (IV.iii.113). Whether Shakespeare was aware of James's toying with the Ralegh conspirators or not, he apparently had sufficient insight into the new King's personality to create in the Duke of Vienna a character who could, for a full act, play with mercy after the fashion of James. Shakespeare must have hoped that here, too, the Duke would seem especially timely to his Jacobean audience and especially understandable to the King.

There are obvious conclusions to be drawn from this exploration of the role of James I in *Measure for Measure*. When the evidence is examined with care, the new King's distaste for the "untaught love" of unmannerly crowds is seen to be demonstrably called attention to, if not in flattery, then at least as an item of contemporary interest. Moreover, Duke Vincentio, though he has been variously identified by contemporary scholars as a stock character in Jacobean comedy[47] and as a forebear of Prospero, in *The Tempest*,[48] is also, and much more importantly, seen to be the figure of a Renaissance prince and autocrat, willfully Jamesian in his views of himself and in his attitudes toward affairs of state. We are forced to conclude that Shakespeare's intentions were deliberate, that he created in the Duke a character whose acts and whose theories of government would be interesting to the new age and its new King because they were so carefully like ones which the King had identified as his own. Negatively, indeed, it would be

[47]Oscar James Campbell, *Shakespeare's Satire* (New York, 1943), p. 127.

[48]Harold S. Wilson, "Action and Symbol in *Measure for Measure* and *The Tempest*," *SQ,* IV (1953), 375–384.

difficult to find *any* comment in this play concerning the "properties" of government and "sufficiency" in office which did not agree rather narrowly with James's personal convictions as of 1603 and 1604. Shakespeare, we may infer, was as consciously (if more subtly) attempting to please James I with *Measure for Measure* as was Bilson, for example, in his flattering repetition of James's opinions in his "Coronation Sermon," or Barlow in his flattering portrait of James's role in the Hampton Court Conference.

These conclusions explain the fact that Shakespeare incorporated a rich background of political theorizing into a comedy in which the ironies resulting from the moral decisions of Isabella and Angelo are the dramatic center. Under the pressures of twentieth-century doctrinaire aesthetic criticism, it would be tempting to stop here, and to regard the role played by James I in *Measure for Measure* as of interest only as extrinsic information concerning both the genesis of one element in the play, and Shakespeare's special reasons for including it. Certainly such information does make Shakespeare seem a bit more alive for us as a person, as we contemplate what private ends *Measure for Measure* may have served for him as playwright of the King's men.[49] Moreover, any newly opened vein of Shakespearean fact adds to the pleasure, to the luxury, of that knowledge of his plays which we admit that we enjoy merely for its own sake. Therefore such additions to literary history, as even the most ardent critic of the intentional fallacy might agree, have a right to be heard.

Yet such literary history as that concerning James's role in *Measure for Measure* is something more than casual

[49]Herbert Howorth, in "Shakespeare's Flattery in *Measure for Measure*," *SQ*, XVI (1965), 29–37, makes further suggestions as to the play's topicality, and suggests its failure to please James.

historical information. It cannot radically alter our sense of the inherent dramatic design of the play, nor our awareness of the subtleties of the scene by scene implications of the play. But it usefully enlarges the possible time context in which the play can exist for us. It gives us a kind of double vision, an awareness of the play today, and of the elements still inextricably and importantly a part of it which have, at the same time, lost the sharp edge of early seventeenth-century implication. *Measure for Measure,* viewed in this way, is seen to reflect the first moments of a changing political order. It is a striking demonstration in drama of the fact that by 1604 the romantic world of Belphoebe and Amoret, of Leicester and of Essex, was quite dead, and that the Jacobean era of self-conscious political theorizing and attitudinizing was at hand. James had published his sketches of the emotional and intellectual boundaries of his new, and less durable, world of divine rectitude, and Shakespeare, though no doubt primarily concerned with realizing a play, had caught some of the essence of this new Jamesian world in *Measure for Measure.*[50]

Shakespeare's new Jacobean comedy, indeed, is a startling departure from the dramatic world of his Forest of Arden and his Illyria. Its Stuart political theorizing must have had a much stronger impact then than now. Our knowledge of the relationship between James's ideas concerning the role of king and those expressed in this comedy permits us to see this. But the sense of immediacy in the political element Shakespeare introduced into *Measure for*

---

[50]As G. B. Harrison observes: "*Measure for Measure* may...be the first play which Shakespeare had written for more than a year.... When read against the background of the later months of 1604, it does reflect the mood of the times quite clearly" (*Measure for Measure,* The Penguin Shakespeare [New York, 1954], p. 16).

Measure has clearly seeped from the play in 350-odd years. And the Duke's omniscience of Act V has lost, with the passing of the early Jacobean era, some of its natural-seeming freshness. In becoming conscious of the ways in which *Measure for Measure* reflects Stuart attitudes toward kingship, we add to our awareness of the effects the play once magnified. We also gain new respect for the inherent power of the play because it survives so well into the twentieth century without such magnification.

The political attitudinizing in *Measure for Measure* is part of the structure of this comedy, and cannot be disentangled from it, whether or not we are able to savor the extra knowledge of its relationship to the once substantial world of 1603 and 1604. The Duke remains to reassure us as the observant outsider, formidable enough to rescue all the inhabitants of Vienna from their folly "like power divine," whether or not we know that he mirrors the predilections of James I. In gaining historical perspective on *Measure for Measure,* we may feel that we are examining its structure as if it were an intricate piece of cabinet work we had unglued. But we remind ourselves that when the raw edges are once more pushed together, we still have a self-contained comedy. A legitimate recovery of historical perspective on the political element in *Measure for Measure* serves to emphasize the basic aesthetic fact that it remains alive for us today because its characters are essentially living not in a period of English history, but in a play.

The historical approach to Shakespeare allows us to view *Measure for Measure* in a fascinating and intricate web of time. But the degree to which this play's historically recoverable meanings can make it more viable for us is very slight. The dramatic vitality of *Measure for Measure* is sustained only because the characters as they live in it make choices among possible alternatives which seem natural to an audience (Jacobean or contemporary), and hold its interest. Juliet and Mariana are alive to us in the play as women who give themselves willingly to men; they may gain in historical relevance for us, but not in vitality, by our knowledge of the Elizabethan legal status of their troth-plights. An Isabella who pleads for mercy and then becomes violently unmerciful, converting her sense of outrage into sick anger, an austere, puritanical Angelo who seeks to violate the chastity of a novice, a Duke of Vienna who chooses to play a God-like role, and to prevent all the usual consequences of human folly except those of Lucio, are interesting and exciting people to us, in their own dramatic right. In essence, they live outside history. We are essentially involved, as audience (as were the Jacobeans, indeed), only in their choices within the play, and where they lead in the play. That is, if this comedy is still to succeed, as I think *Measure for Measure* does, and greatly.

Index

Index